The Rossetti Infant-Toddler Language Scale™

by Louis Rossetti, Ph.D.

Skills	Ages
■ Interaction–Attachment ■ Pragmatics ■ Gesture ■ Play ■ Language Comprehension and Expression	■ Birth to Three

Evidence-Based Practice

According to the Clinical Guidelines of the Royal College of Speech & Language Therapists (www.rcslt.org/resources, 2005) and the Preferred Practice Patterns for the Profession of Speech-Language Pathology (ASHA 1997):

■ Impairment in communication skills, interaction, attention, comprehension, or expression impeded the development of effective communication skills.

■ Assessment and intervention should address skills in interaction, attention, play, comprehension, and expression to support development of an even skill profile.

■ Ongoing assessment and management helps to inform parents, target appropriate intervention and ensure access to appropriate resources and services.

The activities in this book incorporate the above principles and are also based on expert professional practice.

LinguiSystems, Inc.
3100 4th Avenue
East Moline, IL 61244
800-776-4332

FAX: 800-577-4555
E-mail: service@linguisystems.com
Web: linguisystems.com

Printed in the U.S.A
ISBN 10: 0-7606-0713-3
ISBN: 13: 978-0-7606-0713-8

About the Author

Dr. Lou Rossetti is Professor Emeritus of Communication Disorders at the University of Wisconsin Oshkosh. He is an internationally recognized authority on services to infants and toddlers with special needs and their families. He is a frequent presenter at professional conferences throughout the world. He is the author of five books and numerous articles on infants and toddlers with special needs. Lou considers himself first and foremost a clinician. He continues to consult in a variety of clinical settings, including neonatal intensive care nurseries and home-based as well as center-based agencies. Lou is most passionate about sharpening the clinical skills of those working with children under three years of age. Lou has been named a Fellow of the American Speech-Language-Hearing Association.

Acknowledgments

You cannot complete projects such as *The Rossetti Infant-Toddler Language Scale* in a vacuum. I am most indebted to the many children and families I have interacted with over the past 30 years of providing clinical services. I never cease to learn from them. They have shaped my understanding of children with special needs as well as helped me understand to some degree the unique set of circumstances parents and caregivers of children with special needs face. There are far too many families for me to mention by name. I am deeply indebted to each of you.

I have known the co-founders of LinguiSystems for more years than any of us will readily acknowledge.

My comments regarding LinguiSystems can be summed up in four words, "You are the best!" I have worked with numerous publishers over the years. Far and away LinguiSystems is the most author-friendly of all. It has been my privilege to work with you, and I look forward to future collaboration.

Finally, and most importantly, I want to express deep gratitude to my family. My four daughters and Ruth, my wife of 32 years, have been a never-ending source of joy and encouragement for me. I can't imagine a more supportive family!

The Spanish translations for this resource were done by **Sandra Rothschild Pavlovic**, CCC-SLP. Sandra has broad experience as a bilingual speech-language therapist and a translator in both school and rehabilitation settings.

Foreword

"I very seldom administer an infant-toddler assessment instrument in the way it was designed to be given." This statement has been shared with me by numerous speech-language pathologists, early childhood specialists, occupational and physical therapists, and birth-to-three providers from around the country and around the world. It was this statement that gave me the initial interest and desire to begin work on this assessment instrument.

Two important principles dominated my thinking as I developed the scale. First, it must be comprehensive and reliable, yet relatively easy to use. Second, the examiner must have the freedom to determine in more than a single way if a child has mastered a behavior. The spontaneous observation of a behavior, direct elicitation of a behavior and the caregiver's report of a behavior should all carry equal weight when scoring the scale.

The examiner should be allowed to use his or her expertise when assessing, as opposed to relying primarily upon the instrument being used. In other words, the intuition and skill of the examiner should take precedence over the manner in which an assessment instrument is structured. Far too many infant-toddler specialists have told me that they felt their clinical skills must take second place to the strict assessment protocols inherent in most assessment tools.

Assessment is the process of gathering samples of behavior and making inferences about a child's developmental performance upon observed behaviors. Tests should simply help the examiner direct and structure observations. *The Rossetti Infant-Toddler Language Scale* is designed to help the examiner gather samples of behavior and to monitor the child's progress through the developmental areas included in the scale. The child development literature is consistent in identifying communication skills as a highly sensitive indicator of school success. Hence, the results of this scale should be of interest to a wide variety of early intervention professionals. If this scale helps professionals from all disciplines to provide quality assessment services to infants, toddlers and their families, and to structure effective interventions, then it will have fulfilled its purpose.

Lou Rossetti
Wausau, WI

Table of Contents

Introduction

Rationale for Assessment

An explosion of information has occurred in the past ten years regarding the identification of infants and toddlers at risk for or currently displaying developmental delays. A new scope of professional practice has emerged, currently known as *Early Interventionists (EI)*. Many health-related and educational disciplines have effectively collaborated to determine what constitutes developmental delay and to provide for the unique needs of such children and their families. The adoption of aggressive federal legislation designed to improve the developmental outcome of children demonstrating developmental delay further focuses all academic disciplines on the need for early detection and intervention for the at-risk and developmentally delayed child. Further, the need to include the family as a partner in the assessment and intervention enterprise has been acknowledged as an important part in providing effective intervention services. The literature clearly demonstrates that children achieve to a greater degree when the family is involved in early intervention activities (Achenbach et al. 1993, Als et al. 1994, Guralnick 1997).

One by-product of this collaboration between disciplines has been the development of materials designed to assess and remediate delays across developmental areas. Materials that address areas of development such as motor skills, cognition, family issues, and language now exist. Of these developmental areas, communication skills has received the greatest attention as it has been shown to be the single best indicator of developmental performance in children under three years of age (Capute and Accardo 1996, Leonard 1992, Linder 1993, Manolson et al. 1995, Yoder and Warren 1993). The correlation between early communication skills and later school performance is also strong. This relationship between communication and developmental performance makes the early identification and remediation of communication disorders critical. Therefore, significant interdisciplinary attention has been directed toward communication and language performance and expectations in high risk and developmentally delayed infants and toddlers.

Infant and toddler communication assessment tools have historically centered on language comprehension and language expression. As the importance of the preverbal aspects of language (e.g., interaction–attachment behaviors, play and pragmatic and gestural development) have come into consideration, professionals have come to see the need for additional assessment instruments that target these behaviors in children under three years of age. Formal measures to assess the preverbal and verbal aspects of infants' and toddlers' communication development have not kept pace with advances in knowledge about these areas of communication performance. Clinicians from a variety of disciplines continue to search for assessment tools that address both preverbal and verbal areas of language development. *The Rossetti Infant-Toddler Language Scale* was designed to provide the clinician with a comprehensive, easy-to-administer and relevant tool to assess the preverbal and verbal aspects of communication and interaction in the young child.

Assessment of Infants and Toddlers

The goal of any assessment of infants or toddlers is to collect reliable samples of a child's behavior on which to base inferences about the child's developmental status. The examiner is responsible for attaching the appropriate meaning to the behaviors observed during the evaluation. The particular assessment instrument serves as a means of providing structure to the observations made. Using this framework, the examiner should consider several factors during each assessment.

The first factor to consider is that the behaviors a child demonstrates during an assessment on any given day represent only a sample of the child's full range of skills and behaviors. In essence, this sample represents a snapshot of the child's full range of developmental skills. Hence, it is difficult to make long-range statements about a child's development based on a single test administration. In fact, the examiner should avoid doing so. The examiner should keep in mind that the predictive value of tests administered in early childhood is not strong. In general, the younger the child, the less predictive the results of any single test administration may be. Time, spontaneous recovery of function, and maturation are on the child's side. A more meaningful use of test results may be to ask, "Based on the sample of behaviors obtained today, what is next?"

When assessing young children, the examiner will need to obtain information about developmental skills from a variety of sources. Formal test administration is one source of data. Other important sources include formal and informal observation, parent report, babysitter or teacher report, and reports from other medical or educational personnel.

The communication skills of children under three years involve much more than simply noting when the child displays his first word. A significant amount of development takes place prior to the emergence of spoken language. A complete assessment of language ability of infants and toddlers cannot be completed without viewing all aspects of language, both preverbal and verbal.

Description of the Scale

The Rossetti Infant-Toddler Language Scale is a criterion referenced instrument designed to assess the communication skills of children from birth through 36 months of age. The scale assesses preverbal and verbal areas of communication and

interaction including: Interaction–Attachment, Pragmatics, Gesture, Play, Language Comprehension, and Language Expression. The examiner may directly observe a behavior that occurs spontaneously, directly elicit a behavior from the child or use the parent's or caregiver's report to credit the child's performance. Results reflect the child's mastery of skills in each of the areas assessed at three-month intervals across developmental domains assessed.

The Rossetti Infant-Toddler Language Scale assesses the following areas of communication and interaction:

- *Interaction–Attachment*
  the cues and responses that reflect a reciprocal relationship and communication between the caregiver and the child

- *Pragmatics*
  the way the child uses language to communicate with and affect others in a social manner

- *Gesture*
  the child's use of gesture to express thought and intent prior to the consistent use of spoken language

- *Play*
  changes in a child's play behavior reflects the development of representational thought symbolically displayed through play

- *Language Comprehension*
  the child's understanding of verbal language with and without linguistic cues

- *Language Expression*
  the child's use of preverbal and verbal behaviors to communicate with others using words

Interaction–Attachment

A mutually satisfying relationship between the caregiver and infant provides an important base for the development of early communication skills. The development of healthy attachment and interaction patterns is dependent on the abilities and opportunities of both the child and the caregiver. If the child is ill or separated from the caregiver for a long period of time, the opportunity and ability to establish healthy attachment and interaction patterns are diminished. Opportunity and ability must be present for both child and caregiver and, if absent or diminished, less desirable patterns of interaction and caregiving may develop.

Healthy newborns show early interaction behaviors, such as establishing eye contact, crying to have needs met, quieting to a familiar voice, and attending to faces and voices. Prior to seven months of age, infants are primarily drawn to faces. The infant's desire to make visual contact with the adult's face is an early indication of adequate attachment behavior. Caregivers smile at infants frequently and respond to their cries and initiate social interactions. Adults can readily set the tone for interaction during these early stages of communication. It is important to help the caregiver of a less responsive infant develop and maintain these desirable interaction patterns. Positive infant and caregiver interactions are believed to have long-term effects on cognitive, social and language skills.

Pragmatics

Pragmatics describes the way language is used to communicate and affect others. Children learn language within the conversational context. The learning of pragmatic rules is set in motion initially by the interactions that take place between the infant and the caregiver. In other words, the child must learn how to interact in a social sense.

The child's pragmatic development continues over time as skills become more complex, reflecting a growing awareness of the rules that govern the use of language in the social setting. The two-year-old child is usually able to participate in a short dialogue with a partner, taking a few turns on a given topic. At this age, the child is also able to introduce a change in the topic of conversation. By three years of age, the child is able to engage in longer conversations stretching beyond a few turns, with four turns on a given topic typical before a new topic is introduced by either the adult or the child.

Pragmatic development contributes to the child's growth in social and interpersonal skills as well as communication skills. Observation of a child's emerging pragmatic skills during the preschool years is a necessary part of any comprehensive language assessment.

Gestures

Gestures are used by children to express thought and intent prior to the consistent use of spoken language and appear quite early for typically developing children. Gestures provide a bridge for the child as he moves from the nonverbal to verbal realm, and they continue to provide communicative support until the child's verbal system is more fully developed.

Gestures should be recognized as a functional part of a child's communication system and their use should be encouraged. A noticeable lack of gestures from a child may be of concern and suggest the child's communication development is at risk.

Play

Both individual and interactional play behavior is assessed by *The Rossetti Infant-Toddler Language Scale*. Play behaviors provide an important way to monitor a child's development of representational and symbolic thought. For symbolic play to develop, the child must realize that a toy is only a representation or symbol of the real object. For language to develop, the child must likewise understand that a word is a symbolic representation of an actual object. Therefore, changes in the complexity of play behaviors usually accompany changes in language use and function in typically developing children.

Changes in play behavior also reflect the development of cognitive skills necessary for the emergence of spoken language. The relationship between cognitive development and language is especially strong in the preschool years. While no one-to-one mapping of language onto cognition is universally accepted, it is clear that certain play behaviors reflect the cognitive skills necessary for the development of spoken language.

Play has an important role in a child's development. The examiner should be familiar with the relationship between play, cognition and language to best assess a child's developmental status and to provide guidance to the caregiver in efforts to encourage the child's development.

Language Comprehension

Age-appropriate language comprehension ability is an important precursor to the emergence of spoken language. Language comprehension involves the child's understanding of verbal language with and without nonlinguistic cues. The child's comprehension development progresses from heavy reliance on nonlinguistic cues, such as gaze, gesture, temporal and situational expectations, tone of voice, and facial expression, to minimal reliance on these cues and a greater emphasis on the understanding of verbal context, vocabulary and words.

Assessment of language comprehension follows this same progression. It begins with observation of the infant's ability to comprehend meaning from nonlinguistic and linguistic cues and continues through assessment of the child's ability to grasp language apart from nonlinguistic cues. The cues given by the examiner during the assessment must, therefore, be carefully controlled to insure it is only the child's comprehension of verbal language that is being assessed.

A child's language comprehension skills strongly impact his ability to learn from the world around him and to successfully function at home, school and in other communication contexts. Any assessment intending to provide a complete picture of the child's overall language skills must devote special attention to language comprehension.

Language Expression

Language expression looks at the child's use of preverbal and verbal behaviors to communicate. An effective assessment of the child's expressive language includes many steps. The assessment procedure begins with an accurate description of the child's expressive language history and a description of the child's current language expression skills by the parent or caregiver. The child and his parents or caregivers are observed as they interact and play, with particular attention given to the child's language productions. The examiner observes the child and also directly interacts with him through administration of formal tests and free play to obtain more information about expressive skills.

Spontaneous language sampling is one of the most widely accepted methods of assessing the expressive language skills of children. It is equally important to collect samples of the preverbal language productions of infants and toddlers and to document the frequency and variety of nonverbal communication attempts. These samples should include ongoing lists of the child's spontaneous and imitated vocalizations, gestures, spontaneous and imitated verbalizations, and any other communicative signals during the evaluation period. These samples provide baseline information about the child's skills and have important implications when planning intervention programs. Parents or caregivers should be encouraged to assist in keeping such lists.

The examiner must consider whether the language performance obtained as part of direct observation and interaction during the evaluation is representative of the child's overall expressive language repertoire. The information provided by the parents or caregivers through questionnaires and direct interviews can be very helpful in making this determination.

Design and Construction of the Scale

The items developed for *The Rossetti Infant-Toddler Language Scale* are a compilation of author observation, descriptions from developmental hierarchies and behaviors recognized and used by leading authorities in the field of infant and toddler assessment. These items were selected because they best reflect current information available about preverbal and verbal aspects of interaction and communication in young children. These items were also considered most representative of a specific developmental skill at a specific age.

As only items that were considered discriminating and representative of a skill at an age were included in the scale, the number of items at each three-month age interval differs. For these same reasons, a child must demonstrate all behaviors for a particular developmental area within an age range before a developmental age level can be considered mastered rather than emerging.

Items are not included at every age range for each of the six developmental areas assessed by the scale. Items are included only when they are considered chronologically appropriate and developmentally discriminating. When the behaviors expected in two consecutive age ranges are very similar, all items are listed at the older of the two age ranges. Items are no longer listed in a developmental area once the early foundation for that developmental area is considered fully established.

Because many aspects of language development overlap and because a specific behavior may signify a child's development of more than one skill, the same test items are occasionally found in more than one developmental area assessed by the scale. These items are cross-referenced under Testing Tips to assist the examiner in scoring.

Throughout *The Rossetti Infant-Toddler Language Scale*, reference is made to the parent and caregiver. The caregiver may be the child's parent, legal guardian, grandparent or any person providing primary care and having primary responsibility for the child. It is the caregiver's familiarity with the child and the child's abilities that qualifies the caregiver to participate in an assessment of the child. In cases where the caregiver is not the child's parent or legal guardian, it is usually necessary to obtain written permission from the child's legal guardian before allowing the caregiver to arrange or participate in an assessment.

In recognition of the increased numbers of Spanish-speaking caregivers, this new edition of *The Rossetti Infant-Toddler Language Scale* includes Spanish translations of all questions directed to caregivers via the Interview Guide (pp. 15-22) and the report questions in the Scoring Guidelines for each scale item under the "Report" heading. This translation is based on Mexican-American Spanish. There is also a Spanish version of the Parent Questionnaire for your convenience.

Note: The caregiver or parent is referred to as "she" throughout the scale. The use of the female pronoun was adopted for consistency of text throughout this manual. It is widely recognized that the primary caregiver may be male or female.

The terms *verbalization* and *vocalization* also occur frequently throughout the scale. *Verbalization* includes the child's expression of true words or word approximations. *Vocalization* includes the child's production of sounds and sound combinations that are not true word attempts.

Finally, all items on the scale focus on the child's behaviors with the exception of Items 5 and 6 of Interaction–Attachment at the 0–3 month level. These two items refer to the caregiver's behaviors. Guidelines are also provided for administration and scoring of these three items in the scoring guidelines section of this manual.

Parent Questionnaire and Interview

Parental Reporting

Parent report provides information about the broader range of skills the child may display in different settings and with different caregivers. The extent to which a child's limitations impact his daily functioning and family interactions is best determined through parent input. Parent report is a vehicle through which the parent or caregiver can express her concerns about the child and her expectations of the assessment process.

The Rossetti Infant-Toddler Language Scale promotes the family's role as a full partner in the assessment process. Parents have been shown to demonstrate the ability to reliably describe behavior in children under three years of age (Rossetti 1986, 1990, 2000). It is the caregiver's interpretation of those behaviors that may be somewhat lacking. Parent or caregiver report receives equal weighting with direct observation and elicited behavior when scoring each scale item.

Parent Questionnaire

Information about the child's past and present interaction and communication skills is obtained through a separate tool called the *Parent Questionnaire* for the English version and *Questionario para los padres* for the Spanish version (henceforth referred to in this book as the *Parent Questionnaire*). Blank Parent Questionnaire forms are included in Appendix B and C. The CD accompanying this book allows you to print copies of these forms as needed for your clients.

The Parent Questionnaire can be mailed to the parent or caregiver prior to the assessment. Provide a stamped, self-addressed envelope to encourage a prompt reply. An introductory cover letter should accompany the questionnaire, listing the name and telephone number of a contact person able to respond to any questions the parent or caregiver may have.

The first part of the Parent Questionnaire includes questions about various aspects of the child's development of communication and interaction skills. A list of words frequently used by young children follows the questions. The caregiver is asked to place a check next to each word her child understands and to circle words her child says. Space is provided for the caregiver to list additional words her child uses. Several items in the Language Expression area and one item in the Language Comprehension area may be scored by using the information provided by this list. A Testing Tip is included for each of these items in the scoring guidelines, making reference to this list.

The completed Parent Questionnaire allows you to become familiar with the developmental concerns expressed by the parents prior to seeing the child. The description of current skills provided by the questionnaire helps to determine the age level at which testing should begin. The listing of other specialists involved with the child may suggest the need to coordinate and minimize duplication of services or to obtain pertinent records from these resources. Each of these factors contributes to a successful assessment and a comprehensive view of the total child, the family and their unique needs.

While the Parent Questionnaire is comprehensive, it should not be considered all inclusive. When a parent's response indicates a possible problem, explore the area in question in greater detail during the parent interview.

Parent Interview

The Parent Questionnaire may also be used as a guide during a direct parent interview. It may be necessary to complete the questionnaire on the date of the assessment if the caregiver has not returned the form by mail or cannot read. Many questions are arranged so that the parent's response to an initial question determines the interviewer's selection of subsequent questions. This arrangement allows the interview to remain focused on the most important aspects of each child's development. (The Spanish translation for the questions is provided in blue type.)

The parent interview is a crucial first step in the assessment process. It is important not to discount information provided by caregivers. This initial contact influences the parent's or caregiver's perception of the entire assessment and intervention process. The goal of the interview is to establish rapport with the parent and obtain needed information. The following strategies may contribute to a successful parent interview.

First, remember that the assessment may cause tremendous anxiety for the parent or caregiver. Give her the opportunity to express her concerns and expectations of the evaluation. Listen carefully to her. A repeated return to a specific topic may indicate the importance of that topic to the parent. Remain in control of the interview at all times, with the overall goal being a balance of parent-directed conversation and your input.

Maintain the posture of a caring, yet nonjudgmental professional. Phrase questions carefully in an open-ended style, discouraging the use of one-word responses. Ask questions beginning with "Tell me about ____," "Can you describe ____?" or "What happens when ____?" Try to avoid using technical terms. Being a good listener communicates to the parent that you are professional and genuinely interested in the parent's observations and input.

The Interview Guide on pages 15-22 is an expanded version of the Parent Questionnaire, incorporating additional questions you may wish to ask in each developmental area assessed. Use this Interview Guide during the direct parent interview. The additional questions are listed under the numbered questions from the Parent Questionnaire. Add to this list of questions as needed during the interview.

The Rossetti Infant-Toddler Language Scale
Interview Guide

Interaction and Communication Development

1. Was your child ever separated from you for a long period of time?
   ¿Se separó alguna vez por un largo tiempo su hijo/a de usted?
   a. *What was the reason for the separation?*
      ¿Cuál fue la razón de esta separación?
   b. *How long was the separation?*
      ¿Cuánto tiempo duró la separación?
   c. *Who spent time with the child during this separation?*
      ¿Quién pasó tiempo con su hijo/a durante esta separación?
   d. *How much time did this person spend with the child?*
      ¿Cuánto tiempo pasó esta persona con el/la niño/a?
   e. *Were parent visits consistent? Daily? Weekly?*
      ¿Sus visitas fueron consistentes? ¿Diarias? ¿Semanales?
   f. *What was the hardest part about separation?*
      ¿Cuál fue la parte más difícil de la separación?

2. Did your child require frequent hospitalization?
   ¿Necesitó su hijo/a hospitalizaciones frecuentes?
   a. *How often was your child hospitalized?*
      ¿Qué tan amenudo fue su hijo/a hospitalizado/a?
   b. *Why was your child hospitalized?*
      ¿Por qué tuvo que hospitalizar a su hijo/a?
   c. *Were any of these hospitalizations long?*
      ¿Alguna de estas hospitalizaciones fue larga?
   d. *What treatment did your child receive in the hospital?*
      ¿Qué tratamiento recibió su hijo/a en el hospital?
   e. *Is your child currently receiving medication? Why?*
      ¿Su hijo/a actualmente toma medicinas? ¿Por qué?
   f. *Do you consider your child healthy now?*
      ¿Considera que su hijo/a ahora está sano/a?
   g. *Where does your child fall on growth curves for height and weight?*
      ¿Dónde cae su hijo/a en las curvas de crecimiento en altura y peso?

3. Did your child resist cuddling?
   ¿Resistió su hijo/a a que se le abrace?
   a. *How did your child react when you cuddled him/her?*
      ¿Cómo reaccionó su hijo/a cuando usted lo/a abrazó?
   b. *Did he/she seem to enjoy other forms of touch?*
      ¿A su hijo/a parecía gustarle que lo/a toque de otras formas?

4. Was your child often difficult to calm?
   ¿Fue su hijo/a muchas veces difícil de calmar?
   a. *What worked best to calm your child?*
      ¿Qué es lo que mejor funcionó para calmar a su hijo/a?
   b. *Did your child seem fussy or upset frequently?*
      ¿Su hijo/a parecía irritado/a o molesto/a muy amenudo?
   c. *How did you feel when you could not calm your child?*
      ¿Cómo se sentía usted cuando no podia calmar a su hijo/a?

5. Was your child often colicky?

¿Su hijo/a tuvo cólicos frecuentemente?

   a. *Describe any feeding difficulties you experienced with your child.*
      Describa dificultades que usted tuvo al darle de comer a su hijo/a.
   b. *Did you seek help? How did you solve these difficulties?*
      ¿Buscó ayuda? ¿Cómo solucionó estas dificultades?

6. Did your child seem very restless?

¿Le pareció muy inquieto/a su hijo/a?

   a. *How did you deal with your child's restlessness?*
      ¿Qué hizo con la inquietud de su hijo/a?
   b. *Did your child have any sleeping problems?*
      ¿Su hijo/a tuvo alguna dificultad para dormir?
   c. *Describe your child's sleeping pattern.*
      Describa los hábitos de dormir de su hijo/a.
   d. *When did these sleeping problems most often occur?*
      La mayor parte del tiempo, ¿cuándo sucedieron estos problemas de dormir?

7. Did your child seem very inactive?

¿Le pareció muy quieto/a su hijo/a?

   a. *Why do you think your child was inactive?*
      ¿Por qué cree que su hijo/a era tan quieto?
   b. *Did your child have difficulty moving around?*
      ¿Su hijo/a tuvo dificultad para moverse?
   c. *Did anything seem to make your child become more active?*
      ¿Alguna cosa hizo que su hijo/a se vuelva más activo/a?

8. Was your child nonresponsive when you "talked" with him/her?

¿No fue su hijo/a receptivo/a cuando usted hablaba con él/ella?

   a. *Describe your child's behavior when you talked with him/her. (Be specific.)*
      Describe your child's behavior when you stopped talking to him/her.
      Describa el comportamiento de su hijo/a cuando usted hablaba con él/ella. (Sea específico.)
      Describa el comportamiento de su hijo/a cuando usted paraba de hablar con él/ella.
   b. *Did your child seem to ignore you when you talked with him/her?*
      ¿Su hijo/a parecía ignorarle cuando usted hablaba con él/ella?
   c. *Did your child turn away or not react?*
      ¿Su hijo/a le dio la espalda o no reaccionó?
   d. *When did your child respond to voices?*
      ¿Cuándo reaccionó su hijo/a a voces?

9. Did your child often avoid eye contact with you or others?

¿Evitó amenudo su hijo/a contacto visual con usted o con otras personas?

   a. *When did your child seem to look directly at people or things?*
      ¿Cuándo pareció que su hijo/a miraba directamente a personas o cosas?
   b. *How did you try to get your child's eye contact?*
      ¿Cómo trató de que su hijo/a haga contacto visual con usted?

10. Did your child often play with toys in an unusual manner?

¿Evitó amenudo su hijo/a contacto visual con usted o con otras personas?

   a. *How did your child play with his/her favorite toy?*
      ¿Cómo jugó su hijo/a a con sus juguetes preferidos?
   b. *Was your child content with only one toy, or did he/she want a variety of toys?*
      ¿Su hijo/a estaba feliz sólo con un juguete o quería una variedad de juguetes?
   c. *Does your child still put most things in his/her mouth?*
      ¿Su hijo/a todavía se mete la mayoría de las cosas a la boca?

11. Did your child use gestures to communicate? When did you first notice this?
    ¿Usó su hijo/a gestos para comunicarse? ¿Cuándo notó ésto por primera vez?
    a. *Did your child try to vocalize in addition to using gestures?*
       ¿Su hijo/a trató de vocalizar aparte de usar gestos?
    b. *Describe some of the gestures your child used.*
       Describa algunos de los gestos que usó su hijo/a.
    c. *When did your child use gestures most often?*
       ¿Cuándo usó su hijo/a gestos más amenudo?

12. Did your child show interest in the people and things around him/her? (Be specific.)
    ¿Demostró su hijo/a interés en otras personas u objetos a su alrededor? (Sea específico.)
    a. *Did your child seem to prefer being alone? Did your child fuss when left alone?*
       ¿Su hijo/a pareció preferir estar solo/a? Su hijo/a se quejó cuando lo/a dejó solo/a?
    b. *Describe your child's behavior when he/she was around other people.*
       Describa el comportamiento de su hijo/a cuando él/ella estaba con otras personas a su alrededor.

Comprehension and Understanding

13. Is your child easily confused when there are many things taking place around him/her?
    ¿Se confunde su hijo/a fácilmente cuando pasan muchas cosas a su alrededor?
    a. *Describe your child's confusion.*
       Describa la confusion de su hijo/a.
    b. *Do noise, bright lights or lots of movement bother your child?*
       ¿A su hijo/a le molestan sonidos, luces fuertes o mucho movimiento?
    c. *Can your child distinguish you or your voice from others in a busy place?*
       ¿Su hijo/a puede reconocerle a usted o su voz de las de otras personas en un lugar donde hay mucha gente?

14. How does your child respond when you give directions?
    ¿Cómo responde su hijo/a cuando le da instrucciones?
    a. *Is it necessary for you to use gestures or point when you give directions to your child?*
       ¿Le es necesario usar gestos o mostrar con el dedo cuando le da instrucciones a su hijo/a?
    b. *Can your child follow two directions in a row?*
       ¿Su hijo/a puede seguir dos instrucciones seguidas?
    c. *Do you need to repeat directions for your child?*
       ¿Necesita repetir las instrucciones para su hijo/a?

15. How does your child respond to simple questions?
    ¿Cómo responde su hijo/a a preguntas simples?
    a. *Is your child able to answer questions that need a "yes" or "no" response?*
       ¿Su hijo/a puede responder preguntas que necesitan de una respuesta de "sí" o "no"?
    b. *Do your child's answers to these questions make sense?*
       ¿Las respuestas de su hijo/a a estas preguntas tienen sentido?

16. How would you describe your child's intelligence or thinking skills?
    ¿Cómo describiría usted la inteligencia y la habilidad de pensamiento de su hijo/a?
    a. *Describe something your child learned to do easily.*
       Describa algo que su hijo/a aprendió a hacer fácilmente.
    b. *Describe something that has been difficult for your child to learn.*
       Describa algo que ha sido difícil de aprender para su hijo/a.
    c. *What is the biggest area of change you have noted in your child over the past three months?*
       En los últimos tres meses, ¿cuál es el área en la que usted ha visto la mayor cantidad de cambios en su hijo/a?

Speech and Language Development

17. Describe the kind of sounds your child made before one year of age (cooing, prolonged vowel sounds, babbling repeated syllables, squealing).
    Describa el tipo de sonidos que hizo su hijo/a antes de tener un año de edad (arrullar, sonidos prolongados de vocales, balbuceo repetido de sílabas, chillar).
    a. *Did your child make attempts to "talk" to you? What did your child do?*
       ¿Su hijo/a trató de "hablar" con usted? ¿Qué hizo su hijo/a?
    b. *How did you respond to this talking?*
       ¿Cómo respondió usted a esta forma de comunicación?

18. Was there anything unusual about the sounds your child made during this period?
    ¿Hubo algo fuera de lo común acerca de los sonidos que hizo su hijo/a durante este periodo?
    a. *Did your child make many different kinds of sounds?*
       ¿Su hijo/a hizo muchos tipos de sonidos diferentes?
    b. *Could you tell how your child felt by the sounds he/she made?*
       ¿Usted podía decir cómo se sentía su hijo/a por los sonidos que él/ella hacía?

19. When did your child say his/her first real word?
    ¿Cuándo dijo su hijo/a su primera palabra real?
    a. *What were your child's first words?*
       ¿Cuáles fueron las primeras palabras de su hijo/a?

20. Did your child continue to add new words on a regular basis?
    ¿Continuó su hijo/a aumentando palabras nuevas en una forma regular?
    a. *How often did your child add a new word?*
       ¿Qué tan amenudo aumentó su hijo/a una palabra nueva?
    b. *Did your child frequently use another way to communicate?*
       ¿Usó su hijo/a frecuentemente otra forma de comunicación?
    c. *Why do you think your child was slow to use more words?*
       ¿Por qué cree que su hijo/a fue lento para usar más palabras?
    d. *Did you try to help your child learn new words? How?*
       ¿Trató de ayudarle a su hijo/a a aprender más palabras? ¿Cómo?
    e. *Did your efforts seem to help?*
       ¿Sus esfuerzos parecieron ayudar?

21. Did your child's speech or language development seem to stop for a time?
    ¿Le pareció que el desarrollo del habla y lenguaje de su hijo/a paró por un tiempo?
    a. *When and why do you think it stopped?*
       ¿Cuándo y por qué cree que paró?
    b. *How did your child communicate with you during this time?*
       ¿Cómo se comunicó su hijo/a con usted durante este tiempo?

22. When did your child first put two or three words together?
    ¿Cuándo empezó su hijo/a a poner dos palabras juntas?
    a. *What were some of your child's word combinations?*
       ¿Cuáles eran algunas de las combinaciones de palabras de su hijo/a?

23. When did your child begin to use more complete sentences?
    ¿Cuándo empezó su hijo/a a usar oraciones más completas?
    a. *How long are your child's sentences now?*
       ¿Qué tan largas son las oraciones de su hijo/a ahora?
    b. *Does your child put endings on some words, such as* walking*?*
       ¿Su hijo/a le pone finales a algunas palabras, como "caminando"?

24. How many different words is your child saying now?
    ¿Cuántas palabras diferentes dice su hijo/a ahora?
    a. *Does your child imitate these words or say them by himself/herself?*
       ¿Su hijo/a imita estas palabras o las dice por sí solo/a?
    b. *Does your child use action words?*
       ¿Su hijo/a usa palabras que muestran acción (verbos)?
    c. *Is your child able to name many objects, people and places?*
       ¿Su hijo/a puede nombrar mucho objetos, personas y lugares?
    d. *Does your child use the same word for many different objects?*
       ¿Su hijo/a usa la misma palabra para muchos objetos diferentes?

25. Do you consider your child to be talkative or quiet?
    ¿Considera que su hijo/a es hablador/a o callado/a?
    a. *Does your child start conversations or usually just respond when others talk to him/her?*
       How does your child start/end conversations?
       ¿Su hijo/a empieza conversaciones o generalmente responde cuando otros hablan con él/ella?
       ¿Cómo empieza/termina su hijo/a conversaciones?
    b. *Is your child able to take at least two turns talking about a topic with you?*
       ¿Su hijo/a puede tomar por lo menos dos turnos sobre un tema con usted?
       How long (number of turns) will your child stay on a mutually agreed upon topic?
       ¿Qué tan largo (números de turnos) se queda su hijo/a en un tema de conversación decidido por los dos?
    c. *Is the amount your child talks with others different from the amount he/she talks with you?*
       ¿La cantidad que habla su hijo/a con otras personas es diferente que la cantidad que él/ella habla con usted?

26. How does your child usually let you know what he/she wants?
    ¿Cómo le deja saber su hijo/a lo que él/ella quiere?
    a. *Does your child try to talk in combination with pointing?*
       ¿Trata de hablar su hijo/a en combinación con señas?
    b. *Does anyone in the family talk for your child or interpret his/her gestures?*
       ¿Alguien de su familia habla por su hijo/a o interpreta sus señas?

27. Has your child ever talked better than he/she does now?
    ¿Ha hablado su hijo/a alguna vez mejor de lo que habla ahora?
    a. *What do you think caused your child's speech to become worse?*
       ¿Qué cree usted que causó que el habla de su hijo/a se empeore?
    b. *Describe how your child's speech is different.*
       Describa en que forma es diferente el habla de su hijo/a.

28. Do you think your child's speech is normal for his/her age?
    ¿Cree que el habla de su hijo/a es normal para su edad?
    a. *How well do you understand your child?*
       ¿Qué tan bien le entiende a su hijo/a?
    b. *How well do people outside of the family understand your child?*
       ¿Qué tan bien le entienden a su hijo/a personas fuera de la familia?
    c. *How does your child react if others don't understand him/her?*
       ¿Cómo reacciona su hijo/a si otros no lo/a entienden?

29. Do you have any concern about the way your child's mouth or tongue works for speech or eating?
    ¿Tiene alguna preocupación acerca de la manera que funciona la lengua o boca de su hijo/a para el habla o comer?
    a. *Has your child had any problems with sucking, chewing, swallowing, or drooling?*
       ¿Ha tenido dificultades su hijo/a al succionar, masticar, tragar o babear?

30. What concerns you most about your child's speech or language skills now?
    En este momento, ¿qué le preocupa más sobre las habilidades del habla y lenguaje de su hijo/a?
    a. *Have other family members or caregivers expressed any concerns?*
       ¿Han expresado preocupación otros miembros de la familia o personas que le cuidan a su hijo/a?

31. What have you done to help your child learn to talk?
    ¿Qué ha hecho usted para ayudarle a su hijo/a a aprender a hablar?
    a. *What worked best?*
       ¿Qué funcionó mejor?
    b. *Do you feel these efforts have helped?*
       ¿Siente que estos esfuerzos han ayudado?
    c. *Does your child seem to enjoy this help?*
       ¿A su hijo/a parece gustarle esta ayuda?

32. Has anything about your child's speech or language development seemed unusual to you?
    ¿Le ha parecido fuera de lo normal algo en el desarrrollo del habla o lenguaje de su hijo/a?
    a. *If so, what?*
       ¿Si es así, qué?

33. How much time does your child spend with other children?
    ¿Cuánto tiempo pasa su hijo/a con otros niños?
    a. *Is your child in a day care or preschool setting?*
       ¿Su hijo/a va a un lugar como una guardería o escuela pre-escolar?
    b. *What age children does your child prefer to play with?*
       ¿Con niños de qué edad prefiere jugar su hijo/a?
    c. *Describe how your child plays with other children.*
       Describa cómo juega su hijo/a con otros niños.

34. Has anyone in your family had any speech or language problem?
    ¿Alguien en su familia ha tenido algun problema del habla o lenguaje?
    a. *Did this person receive speech or language therapy?*
       ¿Esta persona recibió terapia del habla o lenguaje?

35. List any other specialists who have seen your child.
    Nombre otros especialistas que han visto a su hijo/a.
    a. *What information did these specialists give you about your child?*
       ¿Qué información le dieron estos especialistas acerca de su hijo/a?
    b. *Did they make any specific recommendations? (Be specific.)*
       ¿Le hicieron recomendaciones específicas? (Sea específico.)
    c. *How do you feel about what they said?*
       ¿Cómo se siente usted acerca de lo que ellos dijeron?
    d. *What have you done about these recommendations?*
       ¿Qué ha hecho usted acerca de estas recomendaciones?
    e. *Are you scheduled to return to see these specialists again?*
       ¿Tiene cita para ver a estos especialistas otra vez?
    f. *Would you like a copy of the information obtained from today's visit sent to anyone?*
       ¿Quisiera que se le mande a alguien una copia de la información obtenida hoy día?

36. What information about your child would you most like to get from this evaluation?
    ¿Qué información sobre su hijo/a le gustaría obtener de esta evaluación?

Listed below are words that infants and toddlers might understand or say.

• Please put a check (✓) beside those words you think your child understands.
• Circle the words your child says when he/she talks to you.

all	church	go bed	mine	sock
all gone	clock	go bye-bye	more	spoon
apple	coat	go night-night	more cookie	stick
arms	cold	go out	mouth	stop
baby	comb	grandma	night-night	stove
babysitter's name	cookie	grandpa	no	swing
ball	cracker	gum	nose	teeth
balloon	cup	hair	old	thank you
banana	dada / daddy	hands	on	thirsty
bear (teddy)	diaper	hat	out	tired
belly / tummy	dirty	hi	paper	toes
big	dog / doggie	horse / horsie	phone	toy
bike	don't	hot	pizza	truck
bird	done	hot dog	please	TV
book	down	huh?	potty	uh-oh
boots	drink	I	purse	under
boy	ears	in	rock	up
bug	eat	key	see	want
bunny	eat cookie	Kleenex	shhhh	wet
bye / bye-bye	eyes	legs	shirt	what
candy	fall down	little	shoe	what's that
car	feet	mama / mommy	sit / sit down	yes
cat / kitty	fingers	McDonald's	sky	you
chair	flower	me	sleep	yucky
cheese	girl	milk	snow	
choo-choo	go	mine	so big	

Tell me the names of family members, friends or pets your child says.

Tell me any other words your child says.

Abajo hay una lista de palabras que infantes y bebes dicen.

Por favor, ponga una palomita (✓) al lado de las palabras que usted cree que su hijo/a entiende.
Dibuje un círculo alrededor de las palabras que su hijo/a dice cuando habla con usted.

a?	chamarra / chaqueta	hola	nombre de la niñera	reloj
abajo	chicle / goma	iglesia	oídos	salir
abuelita	chu-chu	insecto	ojos	sed
abuelito	cielo	ir	oso (de peluche)	shhhh
acabé / terminé	cocina / estufa	ir a dormir	pájaro	sí
adentro	columpio	ir cama	palo	sientate
adiós / chao	comer	jugo	pañal	silla
afuera	comer galleta	juguete	pañuelo	sopa
agua	conejo	leche	papá / papi	sucio
arriba	cuchara	libro	papel	tan grande
barriga / panza	decir adiós	llave	para	taza
bebé	dedos	luz	peine / peinilla	tele
beber / tomar	dedos del pie	mamá / mami	pelo	teléfono
bici	dientes	manos	pelota	tía
boca	dormir	manzana	pequeño / chiquito	tío
botas	dulce	más	perro / perrito	todo
brazos	en	más galleta	perro caliente	tú
buenas noches	escusado	McDonald's	piedra / roca	uh-oh
caballo / caballito	feo	mira	piernas	ver
caer	flor	mío	pies	viejo
calcetín / media	frío	mojado	pizza	yo
caliente	galleta	naríz	plátano	zapato
camión / troca	gato	nieve	por favor	
camisa	globo (bomba)	niña	qué	
cansado	gorra / sombrero	niño	qué es	
carro / coche	gracias	no	queso	
cartera	grande	no hay	quiero	

Digame los nombres de familiares, amigos o mascotas que su hijo/a dice.

Digame otras palabras que su hijo/a dice.

Administration

Examiner Qualifications

The Rossetti Infant-Toddler Language Scale is designed for use by any member of the infant-toddler assessment or intervention team regardless of primary academic discipline. It is not designated for use primarily by speech-language pathologists. It may be administered by a single administrator or as part of a multi- or transdisciplinary-team assessment. The examiner(s) should have a thorough knowledge of child development and communication skills but need not be a specialist in communication / language assessment. The behaviors included in each developmental area on the scale are well-defined. Guidelines for administration and scoring are provided for each item in the scoring guidelines section of this manual, pages 27-187. Prior to testing, the examiner should review the test items listed at each age range on the scale so that testing can proceed smoothly with minimal need to refer to the test protocol.

Testing Environment

The Rossetti Infant-Toddler Language Scale may be administered in the home, diagnostic center, school, clinic, or hospital setting. The surroundings should be comfortable and appealing to the child with a minimum of visual distractions and noise. The child's primary caregiver should be present to insure the child's comfort and to report and comment on the child's behavior.

The goal throughout testing is to encourage the occurrence of specific behaviors from the child rather than to control how a behavior is obtained. The test environment can contribute to the achievement of this goal. In test settings outside the home, a child-sized table and chair, a large floor mat and a high chair should be available to allow you to adjust the style of assessment to each child's needs. Low chairs with adult-scale seats and backs should be available for adult comfort. A free-play area stocked with a variety of toys should be part of or adjacent to the area where direct testing occurs. Arrange the toys on shelves and in toy chests to help organize this area. A speaker system and one-way mirror in this area will allow you to monitor the child's interactions with the caregiver or other children without the child's awareness.

Consider the needs of a family with young children when preparing the testing center. Designate an area of the reception or waiting room for play and stock this area with child-sized furniture and a selection of toys for all ages. A bathroom should be nearby with an area designed for changing diapers. Have a supply of diapers, plastic bags for diaper disposal, baby wipes, hand wipes, disposable baby bottles, apple juice, paper cups, and tissues available.

Take safety precautions in all rooms accessible to children. Install child-proof covers for electrical outlets and block access to radiators or other heating systems. Shelving and furniture should be stable so that they are not easily tipped over by an active child. The toys in the free-play area should not contain small pieces a child may swallow. A first-aid kit should also be available.

To maintain a healthy environment, arrange to have the area cleaned regularly. Thoroughly clean assessment materials used after each appointment. Keep a supply of soap, detergent, dish towels, and disinfectant for this use.

Before the Assessment

Prior to the assessment, review the completed Parent Questionnaire and other available information about the child's past and current skills to determine where to begin testing. Consult with other team members, and coordinate roles if conducting an arena or multidisciplinary team evaluation. Prepare the protocol and collect all materials needed for the assessment. Refer to Appendix A, pages 195-196, for a listing of materials needed to administer the scale. When appropriate, contact the caregivers by telephone prior to the assessment and ask them to bring a few of the child's favorite possessions and a bottle of the child's favorite drink to the evaluation.

Prepare the protocol by completing the identifying information on the front page of the form and computing the child's chronological age. If the child was born prematurely, also compute an adjusted age for prematurity until the child reaches a chronological age of fifteen months. To compute an adjusted age, subtract the number of weeks the child was born prematurely from the child's current chronological age. Use the child's adjusted age when determining if the child's performance on the scale suggests age-appropriate skills or a developmental delay.

Assessment Procedures

As the evaluation begins, meet briefly with the caregiver to discuss the goals and expectations for the assessment and to clarify questions raised by the initial review of the child's records. Then observe a period of free play or interaction between the caregiver and child, and compile a language sample or list of the child's vocalizations, imitations and communicative attempts. Extensive information about the child's and caregiver's communication and interaction skills can be obtained through this observation. Use this information to score items as "observed" on the scale.

Following the observation period, interact directly with the child to try to elicit the remaining items on the scale. Supplement this information with the caregiver's report of the child's skills. Finally, engage the child directly in free play to complete

the scoring of scale items. Throughout the evaluation, remain sensitive to the child's possible need for a bathroom break, a drink or a short rest.

During the direct elicitation of scale items, make frequent positive comments to the child about his efforts but not about the accuracy of his performance. Smile, speak pleasantly or gently stroke the very young infant as reinforcement. A system of concrete reinforcement, such as blowing bubbles or earning blocks to build a tower, may be used with older children. As the family leaves the testing center, give the child a final simple reinforcer, such as a sticker. Provide the same reinforcer for any siblings present.

The child may be prompted to perform certain tasks as needed. These prompts may include a demonstration of the desired behavior or general comments of encouragement to try a task. The prompts are not intended to be used to repeatedly pressure a child to perform an activity. Once the examination is completed, simply ask the caregiver, "Is this typical of what your child can do?" Add this information to the testing results.

Where to Begin–Where to End

Basal and ceiling levels of performance are obtained with *The Rossetti Infant-Toddler Language Scale*. Establishing basals and ceilings allows you to monitor the child's performance across age ranges for each developmental area. The child's performance within each developmental area yields important information about his patterns of strength and weakness in communication / language development. This information may help determine if there is a need for intervention and has implications for the development of appropriate intervention goals.

Begin the assessment with the Interaction–Attachment area, starting six months below the child's chronological age or suspected developmental level. If all items of Interaction–Attachment are not passed at this age level, testing moves backward in this developmental area until an age range is reached where all items are mastered. This age range is the basal for that developmental area. Once a basal is established, testing proceeds forward until the child fails all items for a developmental area at a particular age range. This age level is the child's ceiling level of performance for that developmental area. Repeat this procedure of establishing first a basal and then a ceiling in turn for each developmental area. It is helpful to identify isolated items passed within individual developmental domains immediately below the established ceiling for the purpose of identifying emerging skills. Such information can be most helpful in determining where to start in intervention.

When testing is initiated at the 0–3 month level or if it is necessary to move back to this level to establish a basal, complete mastery within a developmental area may not be achieved. In this event, testing should proceed forward until a ceiling is reached. The items passed at each age level should be considered as emerging skills although the age level is not yet completely mastered.

When necessary, global basal and ceiling levels may be established to describe a child's performance across all developmental areas. For a further discussion of how to determine global levels of performance, refer to Interpreting Results on page 189.

Recording Responses and Scoring

Each protocol may be used up to three times. Space is provided to indicate the dates of the re-evaluations and to update the child's chronological or adjusted age. Use a different color of ink to score each time the scale is readministered to help differentiate between the child's past and current performance and provide an easy way to monitor changes in performance over time. Enter the age level at which all items are mastered (i.e., the basal) in each developmental area in the corresponding space of the administration section on the front page of the protocol. Transfer this information to the child's Age Performance Profile on the bottom of the protocol in the same color used to score the scale. Use the profile to help describe the child's test performance and progress over time to the caregiver.

Items on *The Rossetti Infant-Toddler Language Scale* are considered "passed" if the behavior in question is noted in one of these ways.

1. *Observe (O)*—The examiner directly observes the child spontaneously demonstrate a desired or comparable behavior. Place a check mark in the *O* column on the protocol next to any scale items the child spontaneously demonstrates at any time during the evaluation. The assessment begins, therefore, the moment you see the child, and you must remain alert to all of the child's behaviors throughout the assessment.

2. *Elicit (E)*—The examiner or caregiver elicits a desired behavior from the child directly. The Scoring Guidelines section of this manual describes how behaviors may be elicited for most items. Place a check mark in the *E* column on the protocol next to any scale items directly elicited from the child.

3. *Report (R)*—When a behavior is not observed or elicited during the assessment, ask the caregiver if the child has mastered the behavior and if the behavior is present rarely or frequently. Suggested questions to ask the caregiver are provided in the Scoring Guidelines for each scale item under the "Report" heading. Two types of questions are provided for many items. The first question is usually an open-ended question. The second question is typically one that can be answered with a "yes" or "no" response. Select the type of question to use with each caregiver based on the caregiver's individual needs. Place a check mark in the *R* column on the protocol for behaviors reported to occur without regard to their frequency of occurrence. Also note how frequently behaviors are reported to occur.

If the child is not yet demonstrating a particular behavior, the box next to that test item on the protocol should be left unchecked.

Language Sampling

An estimate of the child's mean length of utterance in meaningful words is required to score items at older age levels in the Language Expression area of the scale. Attempt to obtain a sample of fifty of the child's spontaneous utterances to compute this mean length of utterance. Try to obtain this sample when the child is engaged in free play with another person. General guidelines for eliciting a language sample during free play are described for each of these items in the Scoring Guidelines.

To compile the child's spontaneous language sample, make a listing of consecutive utterances. Include only those utterances in which all words can be completely transcribed. Include any words, phrases or sentences that are partially intelligible if you can determine what the child's target words were.

Analyze the child's utterances to determine the number of morphemes in each utterance. A *morpheme* is the smallest unit of language that carries meaning. Morphemes include complete words and grammatical inflections, such as the -s in *cats*. Therefore, a morpheme may stand alone or be joined to another morpheme.

Young children frequently use diminutives, such as "mommy" or "horsie," and reduplicated words, such as "bye-bye." These types of words are counted as a single morpheme. If the child is dysfluent and repeats a word within an utterance, such as "I, I, I wanna go," count all repetitions as a single word or morpheme. If the child purposefully repeats a word to stress a message or get attention, such as "Look! Look!", count each word as a separate morpheme. The use of general terms, such as "yeah," may be counted as a morpheme. Do not count interjections, such as "um" or "oh," as a word or morpheme. All auxiliaries, such as "is" or "can," and early catenatives, such as "gonna" or "wanna," count as one morpheme. Inflectional endings, such as plural -s, the present progressive -ing, or the past tense -ed, are counted as separate morphemes.

To compute the child's mean length of morphemes per utterance, total the number of morphemes in all of the utterances in the sample and divide this number by the total number of utterances in the sample. Pages 14 and 15 of the protocol provide a format for compiling the spontaneous language sample and computing the mean length of utterance in morphemes. Page 15 includes a summary of other scale items that may be scored from a spontaneous language sample.

When formal language sampling is not possible because of the child's developmental level, compile a representative sample of the child's spontaneous and imitated utterances and vocalizations throughout the assessment. Note the child's ability to imitate words or sounds upon request. This information is valuable when developing intervention goals and provides a baseline of the child's functional expressive language development to monitor the child's progress over time. The final page of the protocol may also be used to compile this sample.

Scoring Guidelines

Guidelines for scoring each item within the six developmental areas assessed by *The Rossetti Infant-Toddler Language Scale* follow. The guidelines include a repetition of the item as it appears on the assessment protocol and a description of the desired behavior stated as a question. The left-hand column lists any materials needed to administer the item, a description of the procedures to follow to observe or elicit a behavior, and suggested questions in English and in Spanish for obtaining report of a behavior. The right-hand column includes criteria for scoring a behavior as "passed" and any Testing Tips that may assist in administration or scoring of an item.

1 Maintains brief eye contact during feeding

Does the child maintain brief eye contact when close to the caregiver during a pleasurable activity such as feeding?

Observe:
Observe the child as the caregiver bottle feeds him.

Report:
- Describe what your child does while you are feeding him.
  Describa lo que hace su hijo/a mientras usted le da de comer.
- Does your child look at your face when you feed him?
  ¿Su hijo/a le mira a la cara cuando le da de comer?

Scoring Criteria:
The child maintains brief eye contact when close to the caregiver during pleasurable activities such as feeding or when being rocked by the caregiver.

Testing Tip:
When the child is scheduled for an assessment away from home, encourage the caregiver to bring a bottle of his favorite drink to use during the evaluation. This item may be scored in conjunction with Item 2 of Pragmatics on page 41.

2 Shows differing responses to caregiver's vocalization

Does the child seem aware of differences in the type of vocalizations produced by the caregiver by showing different physical responses (may include changes in facial expression or other physical attributes such as respiration, arm or leg movements)?

Observe:
Observe the child as the caregiver speaks to him. What reactions does the child show?

Elicit:
Ask the caregiver to speak to the child using pleasant, soothing tones (4- to 7-word utterances with wide inflectional patterns) for a period of time. Later in the evaluation, ask the caregiver to vocalize in an unusual manner or speak with a sharp tone to the child.

Report:
- How does your child react when you speak to him in a soothing tone of voice?
  ¿Cómo reacciona su hijo cuando usted le habla en un tono de voz tranquilo?
- How does your child react when you abruptly stop talking to him?
  ¿Cómo reacciona su hijo cuando usted de repente le deja de hablar?
- Does your child react differently to different tones of voice?
  ¿Su hijo reacciona diferente a distintos tonos de voz?

Scoring Criteria:
The child changes affect or activity level in response to the caregiver's tone of voice. The child may smile when spoken to pleasantly, widen his eyes or stop all physical activity. He may also frown in response to an unpleasant tone of voice or display disapproval when interactions cease.

Testing Tip:
First attempt to elicit changes in the child's responses to a pleasant tone of voice or to an unusual vocalization. If it is necessary to ask the caregiver to speak to the child in a less pleasant tone, explain the rationale and wait until late in the evaluation to minimize any effect on the child's overall performance. This item may be scored in conjunction with Item 1 of Pragmatics on page 41, Item 6 of Language Comprehension on page 95, Item 13 of Language Comprehension on page 99, and Item 15 of Language Comprehension on page 100.

3 Crying diminishes with adult eye contact

Does the child's crying diminish with eye contact from an adult?

Observe:
If the child cries during the course of the evaluation, observe the child's reaction as the caregiver approaches and establishes eye contact.

Report:
- When your child is crying, what happens as you approach him and look at him?
  Cuando su hijo está llorando, ¿qué pasa mientras usted se le acerca y lo mira?
- Does your child stop crying when you look at him?
  ¿Su hijo para de llorar cuando usted lo mira?

Scoring Criteria:
The child's cry noticeably diminishes when the caregiver looks at him.

Testing Tip:
This item may be scored in conjunction with Item 1 of Pragmatics on page 41.

4 Smiles purposefully in response to caregiver's face or voice

Does the child smile during pleasant interactions with the caregiver?

Observe:
Observe the child as the caregiver approaches him and talks to him in a pleasant manner.

Elicit:
Ask the caregiver to approach the child, speaking pleasantly.

Report:
- How does your child react when he first hears your voice or sees your face?
  ¿Cómo reacciona su hijo el rato que él escucha su voz o ve su cara?
- Does your child smile when he sees your face or hears your voice?
  ¿Su hijo sonríe cuando ve su cara o escucha su voz?

Scoring Criteria:
The child smiles during pleasant interactions with the caregiver.

Testing Tip:
This item may be scored in conjunction with Item 1 of Pragmatics on page 41.

5   Caregiver appears relaxed and comfortable in handling the child

Does the caregiver appear relaxed, caring and comfortable when providing routine care for the child or when handling the child?

Observe:
Observe the caregiver feeding, diapering or dressing the child.

Scoring Criteria:
The caregiver appears relaxed, caring and comfortable when providing routine care and handling the child. The caregiver should not appear tense, worried or annoyed or handle the child in an awkward or methodical manner.

Testing Tip:
The caregiver is more likely to be at risk for caregiving deficiencies with a child who is premature, who has a history of medical complications, who experienced early caregiver-infant separation, who is difficult to console, or who has a handicapping condition. Factors that may put a parent at risk include: early separation, substance abuse, psychiatric history, single parent status, an unwanted pregnancy, teenage parenting, low socioeconomic status, and low educational level.

6   Caregiver smiles frequently while interacting with the child

Does the caregiver smile frequently and respond readily to most interactions with the child?

Observe:
Observe the caregiver's response to the child's signals for attention. Observe how the caregiver routinely initiates interaction with the child.

Scoring Criteria:
The caregiver smiles frequently and responds readily to most interaction opportunities with the child. The caregiver's smiles are appropriate to the situation. The caregiver initiates positive interactions with the child beyond those required to meet the child's basic needs. The caregiver should not appear aloof, preoccupied or unresponsive to the child's communicative signals. The caregiver should not demonstrate a limited desire to touch or hold the child or establish face-to-face contact.

7   Smiles spontaneously to human contact

Does the child smile in response to the caregiver's voice or to interactions other than face-to-face contact?

Observe:

Observe the child as he hears the caregiver's voice or as the caregiver physically interacts with him. The child should not be in face-to-face contact with the caregiver.

Elicit:

Ask the caregiver to move from the child's line of vision. Instruct the caregiver to talk to the child before returning into the child's view, or ask the caregiver to pick up or gently touch the child without establishing face-to-face contact.

Report:

* How does your child respond when he hears your voice but cannot see you?
  ¿Cómo responde su hijo cuando escucha su voz pero no puede verlo?
* How does your child respond when you pick him up or touch him?
  ¿Cómo responde su hijo cuando lo levanta o lo toca?
* Does your child smile when he hears your voice or when you pick him up?
  ¿Su hijo sonríe cuando escucha su voz o cuando lo levanta?

Scoring Criteria:

The child smiles purposefully when hearing the caregiver's voice or when picked up or gently touched by the caregiver. The child should not be in face-to-face contact with the caregiver at these times.

8 Smiles when playing alone

Does the child smile when away from the direct attention of others?

Materials: an infant toy, such as a rattle, a noise-maker or a clear butterfly ball

Observe:
Observe the child when he is alert and away from the attention of others.

Elicit:
Ask the caregiver to introduce a toy to the child. Then have the caregiver move out of the child's line of vision.

Report:
- What facial expressions does your child show when he is alone playing with a toy?
  ¿Qué expresiones facials muestra su hijo cuando está solo jugando con un juguete?
- Have you seen your child smile when he is playing alone?
  ¿Ha visto a su hijo sonreír cuando está jugando solo?

Scoring Criteria:
The child smiles purposefully during solitary activity. The smile should not be the result of attention from others.

Testing Tip:
When the child is scheduled for assessment away from home, encourage the caregiver to bring the child's favorite toy to use during the evaluation.

9 Smiles at faces of several family members

Does the child smile in response to the faces of several family members?

Observe:
Observe the child's facial expression as different family members approach him.

Report:
- Which family members does your child smile at when he sees them?
  ¿A qué miembros de la familia les sonríe su hijo cuando los ve?
- Does your child smile when he sees several different family members?
  ¿Su hijo sonríe cuando ve a diferentes miembros de la familia?

Scoring Criteria:
The child smiles in response to seeing three or more family members other than the primary caregiver.

Testing Tip:
A "family member" may include any person living with the child or a person assuming the typical role of a family member.

10 Stops crying when spoken to

Does the child stop crying when spoken to in comforting tones?

Observe:
If the child cries during the evaluation, note his responses to the caregiver's or other adult's efforts to comfort him.

Report:
- How do you stop your child's crying?
  ¿Cómo para usted el llanto de su hijo?
- Can you stop your child's crying when you talk to him?
  ¿Puede parar el llanto de su hijo cuando habla con él?

Scoring Criteria:
The child stops crying when spoken to in comforting tones.

Testing Tip:
This item may be scored in conjunction with Item 1 of Language Comprehension on page 93 and Item 11 of Language Comprehension on page 98.

11 Shows different responses to family members

Do different family members elicit different responses from the child?

Observe:
Observe the child's pattern of responses with all family members present.

Report:
- Does your child react differently to you than to other members of the family? If so, how?
  ¿Su hijo reacciona diferente con usted que con otros miembros de la familia? Si lo hace, ¿cómo?
- Does your child respond differently to you than to other family members?
  ¿Su hijo le responde diferente a usted que a otros miembros familiares?

Scoring Criteria:
Different family members elicit different responses from the child. The primary caregiver may elicit requests for basic care, such as feeding and comforting. The child turns to the caregiver when in distress or when hungry. Other family members may elicit requests for play or social contact. For example, the child leans toward a family member when he sees a toy previously introduced by that person.

12 Responds to a request to "come here"

Does the child physically respond to the request "come here"?

Materials: an infant toy, such as a rattle, a noise-maker or a clear butterfly ball

Elicit:
Request the child to "come here" while gesturing with extended arms or extending a toy to the child.

Report:
• What does your child do when you hold out your arms or a toy to him and say "come here"?
¿Qué hace su hijo cuando usted extiende sus brazos o un juguete y le dice "ven acá"?
• Does your child respond when you ask him to come to you?
¿Su hijo responde cuando le pide que venga a donde usted?

Scoring Criteria:
The child attempts to roll or crawl toward the examiner or caregiver.

13 Becomes more lively with familiar people

Does the child appear more responsive and active with familiar people?

Observe:
Note the child's activity level and responsiveness with the caregiver when they are alone. Then enter the setting and interact with the child. Observe any changes in the child's activity level and responsiveness.

Report:
• How does your child react when familiar people approach him?
¿Cómo reacciona su hijo cuando personas conocidas se le acercan?
• How does your child react when unfamiliar people approach him?
¿Cómo reacciona su hijo cuando personas desconocidas se le acercan?
• Is your child more responsive when familiar people come near than strangers?
¿Su hijo responde mejor cuando se le acercan personas conocidas en vez de extraños?

Scoring Criteria:
The child is initially more reserved with unfamiliar people, while livelier with familiar people.

Testing Tip:
When you first meet the family, interact with the caregiver for a few moments before directly interacting with or touching the child.

14 Shows some initial separation fear

Does the child show initial fear when separated from his primary caregiver?

Report:
- How does your child react when you leave him with a babysitter or an unfamiliar person?
  ¿Cómo reacciona su hijo cuando lo deja con una niñera o con una persona extraña?
- Is your child upset when you leave him with someone else?
  ¿Su hijo se disgusta cuando lo deja con alguien más?

Scoring Criteria:
The child fusses or cries briefly when separated from the caregiver.

Testing Tip:
Children's responses to separation may vary depending upon their experiences and family routine. The child cared for by a sitter on a daily basis may not show separation fear in this setting. This child may tolerate any type of separation better than the child who spends most days in one setting with the primary caregiver. Consider such factors when interviewing caregivers about separation fear.

15 Shows a desire to be with people

Does the child show a desire to be with people rather than being alone or at a distance from them?

Elicit:
Place the child a short distance from the center of activity in a room. The caregiver should be in visual range of the child. Observe the child's reactions.

Scoring Criteria:
The child fusses or demonstrates signals for attention that diminish rapidly when he is brought into the center of activity.

Report:
- When your child is awake and alert, does he seem to prefer to be with people or is he content to stay by himself?
  Cuando su hijo está despierto y alerta, ¿parece preferir estar acompañado o está contento de quedarse solo?
- How does he show his preference?
  ¿Cómo muestra él sus preferencias?
- Does your child enjoy being with people more than playing by himself?
  ¿Le gusta a su hijo estar acompañado más que jugar solo?

16

Shows sensitivity to others' moods

Does the child seem aware of and sensitive to the moods of others?

Elicit:
Bring the child into face-to-face contact. Speak to the child enthusiastically with facial animation. Later speak to the child in a somber tone with reduced facial animation.

Report:
- How does your child show that he is aware of differences in your moods?
  ¿Cómo demuestra su hijo que se da cuenta de cambios en su humor?
- Does your child show that he is aware of differences in your moods?
  ¿Su hijo demuestra que se da cuenta de cambios en su humor?

Scoring Criteria:
The child responds to differences in the moods of others. The child may smile with an increase in liveliness when presented with an enthusiastic speaker. The child may calm and appear unhappy in response to a somber speaker or cry when a sibling is scolded.

17

Displays fear of strangers

Does the child display an increased fear of strangers?

Observe:
Note the child's responses as he is first approached by an unfamiliar examiner.

Report:
- How does your child react to unfamiliar people?
  ¿Cómo reacciona su hijo a personas extrañas?
- Does your child seem afraid of strangers?
  ¿Su hijo parece tener miedo a extraños?

Scoring Criteria:
The child demonstrates an initial fear of strangers. The child may fuss, cry, withdraw, or turn toward the caregiver.

18 Allows release of contact in new situations

Does the child tolerate momentary release of physical contact from caregiver in unfamiliar situations?

Observe:
Observe the family as it enters the evaluation setting. Note the child's response as the caregiver first releases contact with the child.

Report:
• When you first enter a new situation, how does your child react when you put him down or let go of his hand?
  Cuando entra en una situación nueva, ¿cómo reacciona su hijo cuando lo baja o le suelta la mano?
• Does your child separate from you easily in new situations?
  ¿Su hijo se separa de usted facilmente en situaciones nuevas?

Scoring Criteria:
The child tolerates a brief period of release from physical contact with the caregiver. An unfamiliar person should not approach the child during this time.

19 Performs for social attention

Does the child do something to get the attention of others?

Observe:
Note behaviors the child directs toward the caregiver or examiner when he is not receiving or maintaining the attention of others.

Report:
• What does your child do when he wants your attention?
  ¿Qué hace su hijo cuando quiere su antención?

Scoring Criteria:
The child demonstrates behavior intended to obtain or maintain the social attention of others. The child may produce vocalizations such as a raspberry, pat or pull at a person, perform an action repetitively or move toward a forbidden object.

12–15 Months
Interaction–Attachment

Items are not listed at this age level as it is difficult to distinguish between behaviors typical of the 12–15 month range and behaviors typical of the 15–18 month range.

20   Plays away from familiar people

Does the child play at a distance from familiar people?

Observe:
Note if the child moves away from the caregiver to play with toys during the evaluation.

Elicit:
Ask the caregiver to leave the immediate area where the child is engaged in play. The caregiver should remain in view of the child. Observe the child's reaction when the caregiver leaves the area.

Report:
• What does your child do when you leave the area where he is playing?
  ¿Qué hace su hijo cuando usted se va del lugar donde él está jugando?
• Does your child allow you to leave the immediate area where he is playing?
  ¿Su hijo le deja ir del lugar inmediato donde él está jugando?

Scoring Criteria:
The child continues to play when the caregiver leaves the area, or the child leaves the immediate area around the caregiver to play with toys.

Testing Tip:
Allow the child to become accustomed to the evaluation setting before attempting this item.

21   Requests assistance from an adult

Does the child request assistance from an adult when he is unable to operate a toy?

Materials: wind-up toys, a See 'n Say, a battery-operated toy with a hidden switch, or a jack-in-the-box

Observe:
Observe the child's reaction to toys he is unable to operate during the evaluation.

Elicit:
Consult with the caregiver to select a toy the child is unable to operate independently. Operate the toy once to attract the child's interest. Give the toy to the child. Observe the child's reactions when he is unable to operate the toy.

Report:
• What does your child do when he is unable to make a toy work?
  ¿Qué hace su hijo cuando no puede hacer que funcione un juguete?
• Does your child ask for help when a toy won't work?
  ¿Su hijo pide ayuda cuando no funciona un juguete?

Scoring Criteria:
The child requests assistance from an adult when he is unable to operate a toy.

Testing Tip:
This item may be scored in conjunction with Item 29 of Play on page 84.

22 Retreats to caregiver when an unfamiliar adult approaches

Does the child retreat to the caregiver or show anxiety or fear when an unfamiliar adult approaches him?

Observe:
Observe the child's reaction if an unfamiliar adult approaches and tries to interact with him.

Scoring Criteria:
The child retreats to the caregiver when an unfamiliar adult approaches him.

Report:
- What does your child do when an unfamiliar adult approaches him and tries to talk to him? ¿Qué hace su hijo cuando un adulto extraño se le acerca y trata de hablar con él?
- Does your child return to you if an unfamiliar adult approaches him and tries to talk to him? ¿Su hijo regresa a donde usted si un adulto extraño se le acerca y trata de hablar con él?

✳ ✳ ✳ ✳ ✳ ✳ ✳ ✳ ✳ ✳

18–36 Months
Interaction–Attachment

The early foundation for the development of interaction–attachment is considered fully established at 18 months, so no further items are listed.

1

Responds to adult interaction

Does the child respond to adult interaction?

Observe:
Observe the child's reaction as an adult interacts with her.

Elicit:
Hold, touch or talk to the child. Observe the child's response.

Report:
• How does your child respond when you talk to her or touch her?
  ¿Cómo responde su hija cuando usted le habla o la toca?
• Does your child's behavior change when someone talks to her or touches her?
  ¿El comportamiento de su hija cambia cuando alguien le habla o la toca?

Scoring Criteria:
The child shows an obvious response to adult interaction. The child may smile, quiet, widen her eyes, or stop, increase, or alter her physical activity in any manner.

Testing Tip:
This item may be scored in conjunction with Items 2-4 of Interaction–Attachment on pages 29-30.

2

Seeks to make eye contact with an adult

Does the child seek to establish or maintain eye contact with an adult?

Observe:
Observe the child as the caregiver directly interacts with her.

Elicit:
Ask the caregiver to try to establish eye contact with the child as part of a pleasurable interaction. Note whether or not the child seeks to make or maintain eye contact with the caregiver.

Report:
• Does your child search your face until she is able to make eye contact with you?
  ¿Su hija busca su cara hasta que pueda hacer contacto visual con usted?

Scoring Criteria:
The child establishes eye contact with an adult. The child not only scans the adult's face but searches for the adult's eyes. The eye contact may be brief.

Testing Tip:
This item may be scored in conjunction with Item 1 of Interaction–Attachment on page 29 and Item 7 of Pragmatics on page 44.

3 Laughs at amusing activities

Does the child laugh at amusing activities?

Observe:
Observe the child's reactions as adults interact with her during the evaluation.

Elicit:
Ask the caregiver to describe activities that make the child laugh. Engage the child in these activities, or gently bounce her on your knee or talk to her in a silly manner.

Report:
- How can you make your child laugh?
  ¿Cómo puede hacerle reír a su hija?
- Does your child laugh when you tickle her, bounce her on your knee or talk to her in a silly manner?
  ¿Su hija se ríe cuando le hace cosquillas, le hace saltar en sus rodillas o le habla de una manera graciosa?

Scoring Criteria:
The child laughs at activities that involve another person.

Testing Tip:
This item may be scored in conjunction with Item 4 of Play on page 70.

4 Shows interest in people, not objects

Does the child appear more interested in people than objects?

Materials: an infant toy, such as a rattle or a noisemaker

Observe:
Observe the child's reactions to people and to objects presented to her during the evaluation.

Elicit:
Present a toy to the child holding it at eye level. Note where the child looks and maintains her attention.

Report:
- Is your child more interested in looking at people or at objects? How can you tell?
  ¿Su hija está más interesada en mirar a personas u objetos? ¿Cómo sabe?

Scoring Criteria:
The child shows a greater interest in looking at a person than an object. The child directs her attention more readily to a person's face and maintains attention for a longer time. When presented with a toy, the child shows greater interest in the person holding the toy than in the toy itself.

5

Cries to get attention

Does the child cry to indicate a desire for social contact?

Report:
- How can you tell when your child is lonely or wants your attention?
  ¿Cómo sabe cuando su hija se siente sola o necesita su atención?
- Does your child cry in a special way when she is lonely or wants your attention?
  ¿Su hija llora de una manera especial cuando está sola o quiere su atención?

Scoring Criteria:
The caregiver reports the child cries to indicate a desire for social contact. The caregiver is able to differentiate between the child's cry for attention and her cry because she is wet or hungry.

Testing Tip:
This item may be scored in conjunction with Item 8 of Language Expression on page 138

 6

Produces different cries for different reasons

Does the child produce different cries signaling differing desires?

Report:
- How does your child's cry sound when she is wet or hungry compared to when she is sick or lonely? Is there a difference?
  ¿Cómo suena el llanto de su hija cuando está mojada o tiene hambre, comparado con el llanto cuando está enferma o sola? ¿Hay diferencia?
- Does your child's cry sound different when she is hungry or wet compared to when she is sick?
  ¿El llanto de su hija suena diferente cuando tiene hambre o está mojada comparado con el llanto cuando está enferma?

Scoring Criteria:
The caregiver reports she is able to distinguish between the child's cries. The sound of the child's cry indicates if she is hungry, wet or ill.

Testing Tip:
This item may be scored in conjunction with Item 5 of Language Expression on page 137 and Item 11 of Language Expression on page 140.

Maintains eye contact

Does the child maintain eye contact with another person?

Observe:
Observe the child as an adult directly interacts with her during the evaluation.

Elicit:
Establish eye contact with the child as part of a pleasurable interaction. Note if the child maintains eye contact.

Report:
• Does your child look at your eyes for brief periods when you are talking or playing with her?
¿Su hija le mira a los ojos por momentos breves cuando está hablando o jugando con ella?

Scoring Criteria:
The child maintains eye contact with another person for brief periods.

Testing Tip:
This item may be scored in conjunction with Item 2 of Pragmatics on page 41.

 Vocalizes in response to vocalization

Does the child vocalize in response to an adult's vocalization?

Observe:
Observe the child's response when an adult vocalizes to her during the evaluation.

Elicit:
Vocalize to the child in a playful manner for a period of time. Note the child's response.

Report:
• How does your child respond when you make playful sounds to her?
¿Cómo responde su hija cuando le hace sonidos jugando?
• Does your child make sounds to you after you make sounds to her?
¿Su hija le hace sonidos después de que usted le hace sonidos a ella?

Scoring Criteria:
The child vocalizes in response to an adult's vocalization.

Testing Tip:
A child's vocal response to an adult's vocalization signals the beginning development of turn-taking skills. This item may be scored in conjunction with Item 12 of Language Expression on page 140.

9 Imitates facial expressions

Does the child imitate a person's facial expressions?

Elicit:
Talk to the child in a pleasant tone at close range to obtain her attention. Smile, frown or stick out your tongue and note the child's reaction.

Report:
• Does your child imitate your facial expressions? Describe what she does.
¿Su hija imita sus expresiones faciales? Describa lo que hace.

Scoring Criteria:
The child imitates a person's facial expressions.

✳ ✳ ✳ ✳ ✳ ✳ ✳ ✳ ✳ ✳

10 Exchanges gestures with an adult

Does the child gesture during interactions with an adult?

Elicit:
Ask the caregiver to describe games the child plays that require gestures in response to what the caregiver says or does. Attempt to engage the child in one of these games. Note the child's responses.

Report:
• What game can your child play that requires her to respond to what you say or do with a gesture?
¿Qué juego puede jugar su hija con usted que requiere que ella responda a lo que usted dice con sonidos, palabras o gestos?
• Does your child gesture in response to what you say or do as part of a game?
¿Su hija usa gestos para responder lo que usted dice o hace como parte de un juego?

Scoring Criteria:
The child gestures during an exchange with an adult. The child's behavior is dependent on the adult's behavior. The child may blow to return a kiss, cover her face and hands as the adult performs the same activity or hold her hands over her head as part of a game.

11 Uses gesture and vocalization to protest

Does the child use gestures and vocalizations to protest?

Observe:
Observe the child's interactions during the evaluation.

Elicit:
Attempt to take a toy of high interest from the child. Note her response.

Report:
• How does your child let you know she doesn't want you to do something?
 ¿Cómo le deja saber su hija que no quiere que usted haga algo?
• Does your child gesture or make sounds other than crying to let you know she does not want you to do something?
 ¿Su hija hace gestos o sonidos que no sea llorar para dejarle saber que no quiere que usted haga algo?

Scoring Criteria:
The child uses gestures or vocalizations other than crying to protest. The child may turn away from a person, push an object away, yell, or whine.

Testing Tip:
Administer this item later in the evaluation. Do not fully remove the toy from the child's hand after the child protests. The child may become upset if the toy is taken from her.

12 Shouts or vocalizes to gain attention

Does the child shout or vocalize to gain the attention of others?

Observe:
Observe the child's spontaneous vocalizations during the evaluation. Note if the child shouts or vocalizes to gain attention.

Elicit:
Place the child away from the center of activity in the testing area. The caregiver should remain in the child's view but not attend to the child. Note the child's reaction.

Report:
• What does your child do to get your attention?
 ¿Qué hace su hija para llamar su atención?
• Does your child shout or make loud sounds to gain your attention?
 ¿Su hija grita o hace sonidos fuertes para llamar su atención?

Scoring Criteria:
The child shouts or vocalizes to gain the attention of others.

Testing Tip:
The parent interview may provide an opportunity to administer this item as the parent's attention is naturally directed away from the child. This item may be scored in conjunction with Item 28 of Language Expression on page 149.

✳ ✳ ✳ ✳ ✳ ✳ ✳ ✳ ✳ ✳

13 Vocalizes to call others

Does the child vocalize to call to others?

Elicit:
Engage the child in play with toys of high interest. Then ask the caregiver to leave the immediate area. Encourage the child to call for the caregiver.

Report:
- What does your child do when she wants you to come to her?
  ¿Qué hace su hija cuando quiere que usted vaya adonde ella?
- Does your child make sounds to call to you?
  ¿Su hija hace sonidos para llamarle?

Scoring Criteria:
The child vocalizes to call to others. The child may call out to another child on the other side of a child safety gate, vocalize when watching a familiar adult approach her home, or call to a caregiver from another room.

Testing Tip:
This item may be scored in conjunction with Item 45 of Language Expression on page 158.

14 Indicates a desire for a change in activities

Does the child indicate a desire to change activities?

Observe:
Observe the child's play with toys during the evaluation.

Report:
- How can you tell when your child is tired of a toy or wants to change activities?
  ¿Cómo sabe cuando su hija está cansada de un juguete o quiere cambiar de actividad?
- Does your child let you know when she wants to change activities?
  ¿Su hija le deja saber cuando quiere cambiar de actividades?

Scoring Criteria:
The child's behavior indicates she wants a change in activities or toys. The child may stop playing with the toy she is holding, reach for a new toy or whine while looking at a different toy.

Testing Tip:
This item may be scored in conjunction with Item 35 of Language Expression on page 153.

15 Vocalizes when another person calls

Does the child vocalize when another person calls to her?

Elicit:
Engage the child in play. Then have the caregiver move out of the child's view. Ask the caregiver to call to the child. Note the child's response.

Report:
- What does your child do when you call to her from another room?
  ¿Qué hace su hija cuando la llama de otra habitación?
- When you call to your child, does she call back to you?
  Cuando le llama a su hija, ¿ella le llama de regreso?

Scoring Criteria:
The child vocalizes when another person calls her.

Testing Tip:
If a child's sibling is present when administering this item, have the child remain with the caregiver and ask the sibling to call to the child from another room.

❋ ❋ ❋ ❋ ❋ ❋ ❋ ❋ ❋ ❋

16 Imitates other children

Does the child imitate other children's actions?

Observe:
Observe the child when she is with other children in a free play setting.

Report:
- Describe how your child imitates other children during play.
  Describa cómo imita su hija a otros niños mientras juega.
- Does your child imitate the actions of other children?
  ¿Su hija imita las acciones de otros niños?

Scoring Criteria:
The child imitates the actions of other children. The child may throw objects or play with toys in a specific way after watching another child perform the same actions.

17 Responds to other children's vocalizations

Does the child vocalize in response to other children's vocalizations?

Observe:
Observe the child when she is with other children in a free play setting.

Report:
- What does your child do when other children make sounds or talk to her?
  ¿Qué hace su hija cuando otros niños hacen sonidos o hablan con ella?
- Does your child make sounds to other children when they make sounds or talk to her?
  ¿Su hija les hace sonidos a otros niños cuando ellos hacen sonidos o hablan con ella?

Scoring Criteria:
The child vocalizes in response to other children's vocalizations. The child may "sing," cry or vocalize to request food after seeing another child sing, cry or vocalize.

18 Initiates turn-taking routines

Does the child initiate turn-taking routines with an adult?

Observe:
Observe the child's interactions with adults during the evaluation.

Elicit:
Ask the caregiver to describe a verbal or gestural turn-taking routine the child initiates with her. Then ask the caregiver to try to engage the child in this give-and-take routine.

Report:
- Does your child initiate a turn-taking activity like sharing a drink with you or playing a game of giving and taking toys?
  ¿Su hija inicia una actividad de tomar turnos, como compartir una bebida con usted o jugar un juego de pasarse los juguetes de la una a la otra?

Scoring Criteria:
The child initiates turn-taking routines with an adult. The child and adult may share a drink or food, give and take toys, "beep" each other's nose, or comb each other's hair.

19 Uses vocalizations more frequently during interactions

Does the child vocalize more frequently now than in the past when interacting with adults? Describe what changes you have seen.

Materials: age-appropriate toys, such as simple puzzles, blocks, dolls, toy vehicles, or a busy box

Observe:
Observe the child's interactions with adults during the evaluation.

Report:
• Does your child vocalize more now when she interacts with you than she did before? ¿Su hija vocaliza más ahora que antes cuando tiene interacción con usted?

Scoring Criteria:
The child vocalizes more. The caregiver reports the child vocalizes during give-and-take routines that were previously silent or initiates more interactions with vocalization, or the child purposefully imitates an adult's vocalizations more frequently.

Testing Tip:
Pause after imitating a child's vocalization or after vocalizing to the child to give her time to respond.

20 Uses more words during turn taking

Does the child use more words than gestures during turn-taking games with adults?

Materials: age-appropriate toys, such as simple puzzles, dolls, toy vehicles, or a busy box, all placed in a storage container

Observe:
Observe the child's interactions with adults during the evaluation.

Elicit:
Try to engage the child in simple turn-taking routines using one- and two-word phrases. Take a toy from the storage container and say "my toy." Then prompt the child to select a toy from the container or pat a doll and say "baby." Then give the doll to the child. Note the child's responses.

Report:
• Does your child seem to talk to you more during turn-taking games now than she did before? ¿Su hija parece que le habla más durante juegos de tomarse turnos ahora que antes?

Scoring Criteria:
The child uses more words than gestures during turn-taking routines with adults. When the adult says "my toy," the child may respond with "mine." When the adult says "baby" while patting a doll, the child may respond with "baby."

21   Points to, shows, or gives objects

Does the child point to, show, or give an object to an adult when it is named?

Materials: age-appropriate toys, such as blocks, balls, dolls, toy vehicles, or toy dishes

Observe:
Observe the child's responses to verbal directions an adult gives her during the evaluation.

Elicit:
Ask the caregiver to select three objects that are familiar to the child. Present these objects to the child. Ask the child to point to, show or give you one of the objects. If necessary, prompt the child.

Report:
• What does your child do when you ask her to show you or give you an object?
  ¿Qué hace su hija cuando le pide que le muestre o dé un objeto?
• Can your child point to, show you or give you an object you name?
  ¿Su hija puede apuntar, mostrar o darle el objeto que usted le nombra?

Scoring Criteria:
The child points to, shows or gives an object to an adult when the object is named.

22   Controls the behavior of self and others

Does the child try to control the behavior of herself and others?

Observe:
Observe the child's interactions with others during the evaluation.

Elicit:
Ask the caregiver to select three toys that are familiar to the child. Engage the child in play with these toys. Use the toys in an unusual manner and note the child's response.

Report:
• How does your child try to control the actions of other people?
  ¿Cómo trata su hija de controlar las acciones de otras personas?
• Does your child use words to try to control the actions of other people?
  ¿Su hija usa palabras para tratar de controlar las acciones de otras personas?

Scoring Criteria:
The child understands she is able to modify another person's behavior. The child may tell another child "no" when she does not want to participate in an activity or say "no" to herself when she sees a forbidden object. The child may use words to indicate her needs, such as "drink" or "up," or shout to get another person's attention.

23 Uses words to protest

Does the child use words to protest?

Observe:
Observe the child's interactions with others during the evaluation.

Report:
- How does your child let you know she doesn't want to do something?
  ¿Cómo le deja saber su hija que no quiere hacer algo?
- Does your child use words to let you know she doesn't want to do something?
  ¿Su hija usa palabras para dejarle saber que no quiere hacer algo?

Scoring Criteria:
The child primarily uses language to protest. The child may run away and say "no." The use of crying to protest may continue but should not predominate.

✳ ✳ ✳ ✳ ✳ ✳ ✳ ✳ ✳ ✳

24 Engages in adult-like dialogue

Does the child use words and jargon to "converse" with others?

Observe:
Observe the child's interactions with others during the evaluation.

Report:
- Does your child try to have a conversation with you? Describe what she does.
  ¿Su hija trata de tener una conversación con usted? Describa lo que hace.
- Does your child try to have a conversation with you using a combination of real words and jabbering?
  ¿Su hija trata de tener una conversación con usted usando una combinación de palabras reales y balbuceo (palabras que no tienen sentido)?

Scoring Criteria:
The child uses words and jargon that sound as if she is talking in sentences. The child takes turns talking with an adult to establish a conversation.

25 Uses vocalizations and words during pretend play

Does the child use vocalizations and words during pretend play?

Materials: a doll, play farm animals or a toy car

Observe:
Observe the child's play during the evaluation.

Elicit:
Engage the child in play. Model the sound of a baby crying, animal noises, or car sounds. Observe the child's subsequent play with these toys. If necessary, prompt the child to make these sounds.

Report:
- How does your child use words or sounds when she plays?
  ¿Cómo usa su hija palabras o sonidos cuando juega?
- Does your child pretend to cry like a baby or make animal or car noises when she plays?
  ¿Su hija pretende llorar como un bebé o hacer sonidos de animales o de un carro cuando juega?

Scoring Criteria:
The child uses language as part of pretend activities. The child may cry like a baby, say "ouch" when pretending something is hot, make animal or car sounds, or imitate environmental noises.

26 Uses words to interact with others

Does the child use words to interact with others?

Observe:
Observe the child's interactions with others during the evaluation.

Report:
- Describe how your child typically interacts with you.
  Describa cómo se relaciona típicamente su hija con usted.
- Does your child use words during most of her interactions with you?
  ¿Su hija usa palabras durante la mayoría de interacciones con usted?

Scoring Criteria:
The child uses words to get her needs and wants met, to direct other people or to request. The use of gesture and vocalization may continue but should not predominate.

27   **Takes turns talking during conversation**

Does the child take turns talking with others during conversation?

Observe:
Observe the child's interactions with others during the evaluation.

Elicit:
Engage the child in conversational play routine. Note the child's pattern of initiating conversation and responding to the conversation of others.

Report:
• Does your child take turns talking with you?
   ¿Su hija toma turnos cuando habla con usted?

Scoring Criteria:
The child shows awareness of the need to take turns talking during a conversation. The child may stop talking when an adult begins to speak or may begin speaking during a period of silence in an attempt to maintain a turn-taking exchange.

21–36 Months
Pragmatics

The early foundation for the development of pragmatics is considered fully established at 21 months, so no further items are listed.

Assessment of gesture development begins at 9 months of age. For more information, see page 9.

---

1   Covers and uncovers face during "Peek-a-boo"

Does the child cover and uncover his face when playing "Peek-a-boo"?

Elicit:
Raise and lower a towel in front of the child's face to initiate a game of "Peek-a-boo." If the child responds with pleasure, place the towel lightly over his face, say "peek-a-boo" and prompt him to remove the towel. Continue the game until the child independently places the towel over his face and removes it. Alternatively, ask the caregiver to engage the child in a game of "Peek-a-boo."

Report:
- Describe how your child plays "Peek-a-boo" with you.
  Describa cómo juega su hija "Dondé estás" con usted.
- Does your child cover and uncover his face when playing "Peek-a-boo" with you?
  ¿Su hija se tapa y destapa la cara cuando juega "Dondé estás" con usted?

Scoring Criteria:
The child covers and uncovers his face with a towel or his hands during a game of "Peek-a-boo."

Testing Tip:
Select a lightweight towel for this game. Have more than one towel available and launder the towels regularly. This item may be scored in conjunction with Item 15 of Play on page 76.

---

2   Reaches upward as a request to be picked up

Does the child reach upward as a request to be picked up?

Observe:
Observe the child's interactions with the caregiver during the evaluation and as the family prepares to leave the testing center.

Report:
- What does your child do when he wants to be picked up?
  ¿Qué hace su hijo cuando quiere que lo levante?
- Does your child put his arms up when he wants to be picked up?
  ¿Su hijo sube las manos cuando quiere que lo levante?

Scoring Criteria:
The child reaches upward as a request to be picked up. The child may be prompted with gestures or verbalization.

Testing Tip:
A child is likely to request to be picked up when he is reunited with his caregiver, when the family moves from one room to another, or as they prepare to leave the testing center.

Gesture

3   Waves "hi" and "bye"

Does the child wave "hi" or "bye"?

Elicit:
Greet the child when he arrives or as he leaves the testing setting. Observe the child's response.

Report:
- What does your child do when someone waves and says "hi" or "bye" to him?
  ¿Qué hace su hijo cuando alguien le señala con la mano o le dice "hola" o "adiós"?
- Does your child wave "hi" or "bye"?
  ¿Su hijo señala con la mano "hola" o "adiós"?

Scoring Criteria:
The child waves "hi" or "bye" at an appropriate time. The caregiver may prompt the child.

Testing Tip:
It may be necessary to score this item through parent report as the child may not respond socially to an unfamiliar person.

4   Extends arm to show an object

Does the child extend his arm to show an object held in his hand with or without verbal prompt?

Materials: small, age-appropriate toys that can be easily grasped by the child, such as dolls, play vehicles, windup toys, books, play animals, or beads

Observe:
Observe the child's interaction with others.

Elicit:
Engage the child in play. When the child selects a toy, prompt him to show the toy to the caregiver.

Report:
- How does your child show you a new or interesting object?
  ¿Cómo le enseña su hijo un objeto nuevo o interesante?
- Does your child hold out his arm to show you an object in his hand?
  ¿Su hijo le estira los brazos para mostrarle un objecto en su mano?

Scoring Criteria:
The child extends his arm to show an object held in his hand.

5

Points to objects to indicate awareness

Does the child point to an object when he sees it?

Materials: a colorful toy or stuffed animal

Observe:
Observe the child's responses to objects of interest to him during the evaluation.

Elicit:
Place a colorful toy or stuffed animal out of the child's reach on a plain wall, door or window of the testing room. Before entering the room, ask the caregiver to ignore the toy until the child shows he is aware of the toy. Observe the child's reaction when he first sees the toy.

Report:
- What does your child do when he sees an interesting toy that is out of his reach?
  ¿Qué hace su hijo cuando ve un juguete interesante que está fuera de su alcance?
- Does your child point to objects?
  ¿Su hijo señala a objetos?

Scoring Criteria:
The child points to an object to indicate he is aware of the object.

Testing Tip:
Pointing to objects in the presence of another person indicates a child has developed a strategy for establishing joint attention with others. This item may be scored in conjunction with Item 11 of Gesture on page 62.

6

Feeds others

Does the child try to feed people or dolls using a fork or spoon?

Materials: play dishes, play food, utensils, and dolls

Observe:
Observe the child's spontaneous play in a housekeeping area.

Elicit:
Engage the child in play in a housekeeping area. The adult can model food preparation, pretending to eat food with a spoon or fork or feeding dolls with utensils. Observe the child's subsequent play. If necessary, prompt the child to feed the dolls.

Report:
• How does your child feed his dolls when he plays "dinner time"?
  ¿Cómo les alimenta su hijo a sus muñecos cuando juega que es hora de la comida?
• Does your child try to feed you or his dolls using a fork or spoon?
  ¿Su hijo trata de alimentarle a usted a o sus muñecos usando un tenedor o una cuchara?

Scoring Criteria:
The child places a cooking or eating utensil to the mouth of a doll or person.

7

Combs or brushes hair

Does the child try to comb or brush a doll's hair, his hair or another person's hair?

Materials: dolls with hair, combs, brushes, and a mirror

Observe:
Observe the child's spontaneous play with dolls and grooming items.

Elicit:
Engage the child in play with dolls and grooming items. Model combing and brushing a doll's hair. Observe the child's play. If necessary, prompt the child to comb the doll's hair or his hair.

Report:
• Describe how your child tries to help with his own grooming.
  Describa cómo trata de ayudar su hijo con su arreglo propio.
• Does your child try to comb a doll's hair, his hair or your hair?
  ¿Su hijo trata de cepillar el pelo de un muñeco, el pelo de él o su pelo?

Scoring Criteria:
The child tries to comb or brush a doll's hair, his hair or another person's hair.

8

Brushes teeth

Does the child try to brush his teeth independently?

Report:
• What does your child do when you give him a toothbrush?
  ¿Qué hace su hijo cuando le da un cepillo de dientes?
• Does your child try to brush his teeth by himself?
  ¿Su hijo trata de cepillarse los dientes él solo?

Scoring Criteria:
The child tries to brush his teeth independently. The parent may prompt the child.

9

Hugs dolls, animals or people

Does the child hug dolls, animals or people?

Materials: dolls or stuffed animals

Observe:
Observe the child's spontaneous play with dolls and his interactions with the caregiver during the evaluation.

Elicit:
Engage the child in play with dolls or stuffed animals. Model hugging the doll or animal. Observe the child's play with similar toys. If necessary, prompt the child to hug the doll or stuffed animal.

Report:
• How does your child show affection toward family members, pets or his dolls?
¿Cómo muestra su hijo cariño hacia miembros de la familia, mascotas o sus muñecos?
• Does your child try to hug you, his pets or his dolls?
¿Su hijo trata de abrazarle, a sus mascotas o a sus muñecos?

Scoring Criteria:
The child hugs dolls, animals or people.

10

Shakes head "no"

Does the child shake his head "no" to reject an object, activity or person?

Observe:
Observe the child's interactions with the caregiver during the evaluation. Note if he shakes his head "no."

Elicit:
Ask questions or make requests of the child likely to elicit a "no" response. Observe how the child responds. Prompt the child by modeling a "no" head shake if needed.

Report:
• How does your child show you he doesn't want something?
¿Cómo le muestra su hijo que no quiere algo?
• Does your child shake his head "no" when he doesn't want something?
¿Su hijo niega con la cabeza cuando no quiere algo?

Scoring Criteria:
The child purposefully shakes his head "no" in response to a request, question, activity, person, or object presented to him.

Testing Tips:
Questions or requests likely to elicit a "no" response may include asking the child to give up a high interest toy, asking if a doll should go to bed, looking for food or a toy in an empty container, or attempting to repeatedly return a discarded toy to the child. This item may be scored in conjunction with Item 37 of Language Expression on page 154.

Items are not listed at this age level as it is difficult to distinguish between behaviors typical of the 15–18 month range and behaviors typical of the 18–21 month range.

11   Leads caregiver to a desired object

Does the child take the caregiver's hand and lead him to a desired object?

Materials: a colorful or favorite toy or stuffed animal

Observe:
Observe the child's interactions with the caregiver as he discovers objects of interest during the evaluation.

Elicit:
Place a colorful toy or stuffed animal out of the child's reach on a plain wall, door or window of the testing room. Ask the caregiver to ignore the toy and remain seated until the child takes her hand and leads her to the desired object. Observe the child's interactions with the caregiver when he discovers the toy.

Report:
• What does your child do to let you know he wants something that is out of his reach or that is in another room?
¿Qué hace su hijio para dejarle saber que quiere algo que está fuera de su alcance o que está en otra habitación?
• Does your child take your hand and lead you to a toy he wants you to get for him?
¿Le da su hijo la mano para llevarle a un juguete que el quiere que usted se lo pase?

Scoring Criteria:
The child takes the caregiver's hand and leads her to a desired object.

Testing Tip:
This item may be scored in conjunction with Item 5 of Gesture on page 57.

12   Indicates that pants are wet

Does the child gesture to indicate that he has wet his pants or diaper?

Report:
• What does your child do to let you know that he has wet his pants or diaper?
¿Qué hace su hijo para dejarle saber que mojó sus pantalones o pañal?
• Does your child let you know when his pants or diapers are wet?
¿Su hijo le deja saber cuando sus pantalones o pañales están mojados?

Scoring Criteria:
The child gestures to indicate that his pants or diaper are wet. The child may tug at, point, pat, or try to pull off his pants.

Testing Tip:
This item may be scored in conjunction with Item 17 of Gesture on page 65.

13 Pretends to play a musical instrument

Does the child try to play a musical instrument?

Materials: musical instruments, such as a toy horn, a keyboard or a toy guitar

Observe:
Observe the child's play with toy musical instruments during the evaluation.

Elicit:
Engage the child in play with a musical instrument. Model playing simple tunes on the instrument. Observe the child's subsequent play with the instrument. If necessary, prompt the child to play the instruments.

Report:
• What does your child do when he plays with a musical instrument?
  ¿Qué hace su hijo cuando juega con un instrumento musical?
• Does your child pretend to play a musical instrument?
  ¿Su hijo finge que toca un instrumento musical?

Scoring Criteria:
The child handles the instrument appropriately while trying to play music. He may blow into the horn or try to push down the keys, run his hand over the guitar strings, or push the keys on a keyboard.

14 Puts on or takes off clothing

Does the child try to put on or take off clothing?

Elicit:
Remove one of the child's shoes or socks. Untie the lace of his second shoe and prompt the child to remove that shoe, or remove the child's shoes and prompt him to put on his shoes.

Report:
• What clothes does your child try to take off or put on by himself?
  ¿Qué ropa trata su hijo de sacarse o ponerse él solo?
• Does your child try to take off or put on clothing?
  ¿Su hijo trata de sacarse o ponerse la ropa?

Scoring Criteria:
The child tries to take off or put on an article of clothing. The child may tug at his shoes, pull at his socks, try to pull down his pants, or pull off his diaper. He may attempt to put his foot into a shoe or sock or put a hat on his head.

Testing Tip:
Shoes and socks are often the first pieces of clothing children learn to remove.

15 Pretends to dance to music

Does the child try to dance to music?

Report:
- What does your child do when he hears music?
  ¿Qué hace su hijo cuando escucha música?
- Does your child try to dance when he hears music?
  ¿Su hijo trata de bailar cuando escucha música?

Scoring Criteria:
The child dances to music. He may rock back and forth or bounce up and down on his legs. The caregiver may prompt the child to dance.

✳ ✳ ✳ ✳ ✳ ✳ ✳ ✳ ✳ ✳

16 Gestures to request action

Does the child gesture to request action from an adult?

Observe:
Observe the child's interactions with the caregiver during the evaluation.

Report:
- How does your child use gestures to let you know he wants you to do something?
  ¿Cómo usa su hijo gestos para dejarle saber que quiere que usted haga algo?
- Does your child use gestures to show you that he wants you to do something?
  ¿Su hijo usa gestos para mostrarle que quiere que usted haga algo?

Scoring Criteria:
The child uses gestures to request action from an adult. The child may bring the caregiver's purse to her to indicate he wants to leave, place an adult's hand on the switch of a toy he is unable to operate, or put play food to an adult's mouth to try to continue a snack time play sequence.

17 Gestures to indicate toileting needs

Does the child gesture to indicate toileting needs?

Observe:
Observe the child's interactions with the caregiver regarding toileting needs during the evaluation.

Report:
- How does your child let you know he needs his diaper changed or needs to go to the bathroom?
  ¿Cómo le deja saber su hijo que necesita que le cambie el pañal o necesita ir al baño?
- Does your child let you know when he needs to use the bathroom or have his diaper changed?
  ¿Su hijo le deja saber cuando nesecita usar el baño o que lo cambie de pañal?

Scoring Criteria:
The child gestures to indicate toileting needs. The child may bring a clean diaper to the caregiver and then lie on the floor to indicate he wants his diaper changed, or he may pull at his pants or diaper when it is wet.

Testing Tip:
This item may be scored in conjunction with Item 12 of Gesture on page 62.

18 Pretends to pour from a container

Does the child pretend to pour from one container into another?

Materials: toy cups and glasses; a play coffeepot, a kettle, a pitcher, or a carton of milk or juice

Observe:
Observe the child's play with housekeeping toys during the evaluation.

Elicit:
Engage the child in play. Model "pouring" from a container into a glass or cup and "drinking" from it. Note the child's subsequent play with the toys. If necessary, prompt the child to pour a drink.

Report:
- How does your child play with cups and a coffeepot?
  ¿Cómo juega su hijo con tazas y una cafetera?
- Does your child pretend he is pouring from a container during play?
  ¿Su hijo pretende mientras juega que está echando líquido de un recipiente?

Scoring Criteria:
The child pretends to pour from one container into another.

19   Pushes a stroller or shopping cart

Does the child try to push a stroller or shopping cart?

Report:
• Does your child try to push his stroller or a shopping cart at times?
¿Su hijo trata de empujar su coche o un carrito de compras algunas veces?

Scoring Criteria:
The child tries to push a stroller or a shopping cart.

20   Flies a toy airplane

Does the child fly a toy airplane in the air?

Materials: toy airplanes

Observe:
Observe the child's play with a toy airplane during the evaluation.

Elicit:
Engage the child in play. Model flying the toy airplane in the air. Note the child's subsequent play with the airplane. If necessary, prompt the child to fly the airplane.

Report:
• What does your child do with toy airplanes during play?
¿Qué hace su hijo cuando juega con aviones de juguete?
• Does your child fly a toy airplane in the air?
¿Su hijo le hace volar en el aire a un avión de juguete?

Scoring Criteria:
The child flies a toy airplane in the air.

21

Pretends to write or type

Does the child pretend to write or type?

Materials: paper, crayons or a toy computer keyboard

Observe:
Observe the child's play with paper, crayons or a toy keyboard during the evaluation.

Elicit:
Engage the child in play. Model play sequences that include writing or typing. Observe the child's subsequent play with the paper or keyboard. If necessary, prompt the child to write or type.

Report:
• How does your child play with paper and crayons?
  ¿Cómo juega su hijo con papel y crayones?
• Does your child pretend to write or type?
  ¿Su hijo finge escribir o tipear?

Scoring Criteria:
The child pretends to write or type.

Testing Tip:
Children often try to write when pretending to be a waiter in a restaurant or a parent getting ready to go to the grocery store. Encourage the child to participate in such play sequences when attempting to elicit this item.

22

Pretends to talk on the telephone

Does the child pretend to talk on the phone?

Materials: toy telephones

Observe: Observe the child's play with toy telephones during the evaluation.

Elicit:
Engage the child in play. Pretend the telephone rings. Model answering the phone and having a short conversation. Pretend the telephone rings again and ask the child to answer it. Observe the child's subsequent play with the telephone. If needed, prompt the child to talk by assuming the role of the other person on the telephone.

Report:
• What does your child do when he plays telephone?
  ¿Qué hace su hijo cuando juega al teléfono?
• Does your child pretend to talk on the telephone?
  ¿Su hijo finge que habla por teléfono?

Scoring Criteria:
The child pretends to talk to someone on the telephone. The child may say "hi" or "bye" but is not required to talk at length.

23 Wipes hands and face

Does the child wipe his hands and face with a napkin or a bib?

Report:
- Does your child try to wipe his hands and face with a napkin or a bib?
  ¿Su hijo trata de limpiarse las manos y la cara con una servilleta o un babero?

Scoring Criteria:
The child tries to wipe his hands or face with a napkin or a bib. The caregiver may prompt the child.

24 Slaps a palm in response to "give me five"

Does the child slap a person's open palm in response to "give me five"?

Elicit:
Enlist the caregiver's help before administering this item. Then approach the caregiver with an open palm and say "give me five." After the caregiver responds by gently slapping your palm, turn to the child with an open palm and say "give me five." Alternatively, ask the caregiver to approach the child with an open palm and say "give me five."

Scoring Criteria:
The child tries to slap the open palm of the person saying "give me five" or gives a high-five slap.

Report:
- What does your child do when you say "give me five"?
  ¿Qué hace su hijo cuando le dice "dame cinco"?
- Does your child slap your palm when you say "give me five" and hold out your palm?
  ¿Su hijo le pega la mano cuando le dice "dame cinco" y le muestra la palma de su mano?

The early foundation for the development of gesture is considered fully established at 27 months, so no further items are listed.

1

Plays with rattle

Does the child demonstrate purposeful activity with a toy placed in her hand?

Materials: a rattle

Observe:
Observe the child's actions any time a toy is placed in her hand.

Elicit:
Put a rattle in the child's hand. If necessary, prompt the child by gently shaking her hand and the rattle.

Report:
• What does your child do when you put a rattle in her hand?
¿Qué hace su hija cuando le pone un cascabel en la mano?
• Does your child play with a toy when you put it in her hand?
¿Su hija juega con un juguete cuando lo pone en la mano?

Scoring Criteria:
The child demonstrates purposeful activity when a toy is placed in her hand. The child may bring the toy to her mouth or shake the toy to produce a noise. The child's activity should be more than reflexive and demonstrate purposeful awareness of the toy.

Testing Tip:
Keep a large bin nearby during the evaluation. Place test objects in the bin after the child uses them during testing. Use the bin to transport the objects for cleaning before they are used with another child.

2

Momentarily looks at objects

Does the child look at objects for a brief period?

Materials: an infant toy, such as a rattle or a noisemaker

Observe:
Observe the child when the caregiver places objects so the child can see or touch them. Note if the child visually attends to any object within the room.

Elicit:
Place a toy where the child can see or touch it.

Report:
• How does your child react when you first show her a toy?
¿Cómo reacciona su hija cuando le muestra un juguete por primera vez?
• Does your child seem to notice new or familiar objects within a room?
¿Su hija parece darse cuenta de objetos nuevos o familiares en una habitación?

Scoring Criteria:
The child looks at new or familiar objects within a room or at items placed within visual range. The child should begin to attend to objects as opposed primarily to faces and people.

Testing Tip:
Limit the number of high interest wall hangings or pictures in the immediate evaluation area as the child may become overstimulated.

Play

0–3 Months
Play

3   Attempts to imitate facial expressions

Does the child attempt to imitate the facial expressions of a familiar adult?

Elicit:
Ask the caregiver to engage the child in highly animated face-to-face contact. Instruct the caregiver to use exaggerated facial movements during the interaction.

Report:
• Does your child imitate your facial expressions at times? Describe what she does.
¿Su hija imita algunas veces sus expresiones faciales? Describa lo que hace.

Scoring Criteria:
The child attempts to imitate the facial expressions of a familiar adult. The child may widen her eyes or protrude her lips.

※ ※ ※ ※ ※ ※ ※ ※ ※ ※

3–6 Months
Play

4   Enjoys frolic play

Does the child show pleasure in response to frolic play?

Elicit:
Engage the child in frolic play. Tickle the child, bounce her on a knee, hold her in the air, or gently shake her arms from side to side.

Report:
• How does your child react when you tickle her, bounce her on your knee or hold her in the air?
¿Cómo reacciona su hija cuando le hace cosquillas, la hace saltar en su rodilla o la tiene en el aire?
• Does your child show pleasure when you play with her?
¿Su hija le demuestra placer cuando usted juega con ella?

Scoring Criteria:
The child smiles, laughs or shows other signs of pleasure in response to frolic play.

Testing Tip:
This item may be scored in conjunction with Item 3 of Pragmatics on page 42.

5

Smiles at self in a mirror

Does the child show interest in or smile at her image in a mirror?

Materials: a mirror

Elicit:
Hold a mirror at the child's eye level and prompt the child to look in the mirror.

Report:
• What does your child do when she sees herself in the mirror?
  ¿Qué hace su hija cuando se ve en el espejo?
• Does your child like to see herself in the mirror?
  ¿A su hija le gusta verse en el espejo?

Scoring Criteria:
The child smiles at her image in a mirror.

Testing Tip:
As a safety measure, use unbreakable mirrors with guarded corners and edges. This item may be scored in conjunction with Item 12 of Play on page 75.

6

Reaches for objects

Does the child reach for nearby objects?

Materials: an infant toy, such as a rattle; a noisemaker; a clear butterfly ball; or a baby bottle

Observe:
Observe the child as the caregiver brings toys, interesting objects or food into close view and within reach.

Elicit:
Bring toys, high interest objects or food into the child's view and within reach.

Report:
• What does your child do when she sees something she wants nearby?
  ¿Qué hace su hija cuando ve algo cercano que quiere?
• Does your child try to reach objects she sees?
  ¿Su hija trata de alcanzar objetos que ve?

Scoring Criteria:
The child reaches for nearby objects.

Testing Tip:
Consult with the caregiver before including food as part of any activity. Use only foods the child is allowed to eat. The child may become frustrated if she is not allowed to have the food at the end of the activity.

7 Bangs objects in play

Does the child bang objects during play?

Materials: an infant toy the child is able to grasp firmly, such as a spoon, a rattle with a handle, or a plastic ring; a flat, solid surface, such as a high chair tray

Observe:
Observe the child when she is seated and holding a toy. Observe the child when she is seated with a flat, solid surface in front of her.

Elicit:
Secure the child in a sitting position. Place an object in the child's hand or place her hand on a flat, solid surface. Grasp the child's hand and bang the object or gently tap the child's hand on the solid surface to prompt banging.

Report:
- How does your child play with objects that she can hold in her hand?
  ¿Cómo juega su hija con objetos que puede sostener en la mano?
- Does your child ever bang with objects when she is playing?
  ¿Su hija alguna vez golpea con objetos cuando está jugando?

Scoring Criteria:
The child independently bangs objects or pounds her hand on a surface.

Smiles and laughs during games

Does the child smile and laugh at games such as "Patty-cake" and "Peek-a-boo"?

Elicit:
Initiate a game such as "Patty-cake" or "Peek-a-boo" with the child. Prompt the child to participate in the game.

Scoring Criteria:
The child smiles and laughs at games such as "Patty-cake" and "Peek-a-boo."

Report:
• How does your child react when you play a game like "Patty-cake" or "Peek-a-boo" with her?
¿Cómo reacciona su hija cuando usted juega juegos como "Dónde estás", "Tortillitas" o "Aserrín, aserrán" con ella?
• Does your child like to play games like "Patty-cake" or "Peek-a-boo"?
¿A su hija le gusta jugar juegos como "Dónde estás", "Tortillitas" o "Aserrín, aserrán"?

Participates in games with adults

Does the child attempt to cooperate in a turn-taking routine in simple games with an adult?

Materials: a ball or cup

Elicit:
Introduce a simple, cooperative game, such as rolling a ball, taking and giving a drink or playing "Peek-a-boo." Prompt the child to take a turn in the game.

Scoring Criteria:
The child displays reciprocal behavior in play by rolling a ball back and forth, putting a cup to an adult's mouth or taking a turn in "Peek-a-boo."

Report:
• Which games can your child play where she tries to take turns with you?
¿Qué juegos juega su hija con usted en los que trata de tomar turnos?
• Does your child take turns rolling a ball back and forth or playing "Peek-a-boo" with you, or engage in any comparable turn-taking routine?
¿Su hija toma turnos rodando una pelota de ella a usted o jugando "Dónde estás" con usted, o toma parte en otros juegos comparables donde se toman turnos?

10 Demonstrates anticipation of play activities

Does the child show excitement in anticipation of a play activity?

Materials: a small, brightly colored stuffed animal or doll

Elicit:
Approach and lightly tickle the child with a stuffed animal, a doll or your fingers to elicit a pleasurable reaction. Repeat this sequence. Note the child's reaction as she is approached but not yet in contact with you or the toy.

Report:
• How does your child react when she knows you want to play?
 ¿Cómo reacciona su hija cuando sabe que usted quiere jugar?
• Does your child appear excited when you show her a toy and want to play?
 ¿Su hija parece entusiasmada cuando usted le muestra un juguete y quiere jugar?

Scoring Criteria:
The child demonstrates anticipation of play activities. The child may laugh, smile, vocalize, or show increased physical activity.

11 Searches for hidden objects

Does the child search for toys that are placed out of her sight?

Materials: a familiar infant toy, such as a rattle, a noisemaker or a clear butterfly ball

Observe:
Observe the child when an object of interest is placed or falls out of sight.

Elicit:
Select an object of high interest to the child. Prompt the child to look at the object. Then place the object out of sight but in the immediate area.

Report:
• What does your child do when she is playing with a toy and it falls out of sight?
 ¿Qué hace su hija cuando está jugando con un juguete y se le cae donde no puede verlo?
• Does your child look for toys that disappear from sight?
 ¿Su hija busca juguetes que desaparecen fuera de su vista?

Scoring Criteria:
The child actively searches for the object after it has been placed or has fallen out of sight. The child may visually scan in the direction of the object or move toward the spot where the object was last seen, or protest in some manner at the loss of the object.

12

Reaches for self in a mirror

Does the child reach for her image in a mirror?

Materials: a mirror

Elicit:
Hold a mirror at the child's eye level. Prompt the child to look in the mirror.

Report:
• What does your child do when she sees herself in a mirror?
  ¿Qué hace su hija cuando se ve en el espejo?
• Does your child try to touch her image in the mirror?
  ¿Su hija trata de tocar su imagen en el espejo?

Scoring Criteria:
The child reaches for, attempts to kiss or pats her image in the mirror.

Testing Tip:
This item may be scored in conjunction with Item 5 of Play on page 71.

13

Interacts with objects without mouthing or banging

Does the child interact with objects other than by mouthing or banging them?

Materials: infant toys, such as a noisemaker, a ball, a cup, a bell, blocks, a squeeze toy, or a pull-and-push toy

Observe:
Observe the child as she interacts with toys.

Report:
• Describe how your child plays with toys.
  Describa cómo juega su hija con juguetes.
• Does your child put toys in her mouth or bang them on the floor or table?
  ¿Su hija se mete los juguetes a la boca o los golpea contra el suelo o la mesa?

Scoring Criteria:
The child demonstrates play strategies such as visually examining, shaking, pushing, or placing one object inside another. These behaviors may occur in combination with mouthing and banging objects.

14

Participates in speech-routine games

Does the child respond through movement to speech-routine games?

Elicit:
Ask the caregiver for examples of the child's favorite speech-routine games. These games may include "So Big" or "Patty-cake;" finger plays, such as "Where Is Thumbkin?"; simple songs; or a playful *yes/no* interaction, such as "Is this your nose?" Initiate a speech-routine game with the child. Prompt the child to participate.

Report:
- How does your child react when you play a familiar speech game like "So Big" or "Patty-cake"?
  ¿Cómo reacciona su hija cuando juega con ella un juego conocido de palabras como "Tortillitas" o "Aserrín, aserrán"?
- Does your child like to play games like "So Big" and "Patty-cake"?
  ¿A su hija le gusta jugar juegos como "Tortillitas" o "Aserrín, aserrán"?

Scoring Criteria:
The child responds through physical movement to speech-routine games. The child may raise her arms in response to "How big is baby?," pat her hands together for "Patty-cake" or vocalize and gesture to finger plays and songs that have accompanying actions.

Testing Tip:
This item may be scored in conjunction with Item 35 of Language Comprehension on page 110 and Item 26 of Language Expression on page 148.

15

Covers face with towel during "Peek-a-boo"

Does the child play "Peek-a-boo" by covering and uncovering her face with a towel?

Materials: a towel

Elicit:
Raise and lower a towel in front of the child's face to initiate a game of "Peek-a-boo." If the child responds with pleasure, place the towel lightly over her face, say "peek-a-boo" and prompt the child to remove the towel. Continue the game until the child spontaneously places the towel over her face or removes it.

Report:
- Describe what your child does when she plays "Peek-a-boo" with you.
  Describa lo que hace su hija cuando juega "Dónde estás" con usted.
- Does your child cover or uncover her face to play "Peek-a-boo"?
  ¿Su hija se tapa o destapa la cara cuando juega "Dónde estás"?

Scoring Criteria:
The child attempts to cover her face or pull the towel off her face during the game.

Testing Tip:
Select a lightweight towel for this game. Have more than one towel available and launder the towels regularly. This item may be scored in conjunction with Item 1 of Gesture on page 55.

16 Resists removal of a toy

Does the child resist the removal of a toy from her grasp?

Materials: small infant toys that can be easily grasped by the child, such as noisemakers, rattles, plastic rings, or small dolls

Elicit:
Present the child with a variety of toys. After the child selects a toy, attempt to remove the toy from her hand.

Report:
• What does your child do when you try to take a toy from her?
  ¿Qué hace su hija cuando usted trata de quitarle un juguete?
• Does your child resist letting you take a favorite toy from her?
  ¿Su hija resiste cuando usted le quiere quitar un juguete que le gusta mucho?

Scoring Criteria:
The child maintains a strong grasp and pulls the toy toward her, or the child whines, cries and turns away from the examiner or caregiver.

Testing Tip:
Do not fully remove the toy from the child's hand after feeling the pull of resistance. The child may become upset if the toy is taken from her.

17 Tries to secure an object out of reach

Does the child try to reach or move toward an object that is out of her immediate reach?

Materials: infant toys of high interest to the child, such as noisemakers, balls, bells, dolls, squeeze toys, or push-and-pull toys

Observe:
Observe the child's attempts to obtain desired toys throughout the evaluation.

Elicit:
Remove toys from the immediate area around the child. Introduce a new toy, placing it just outside of the child's reach.

Report:
• What does your child do when she wants a toy that is out of her reach?
  ¿Qué hace su hija cuando quiere un juguete que no está a su alcance?
• Does your child try to get a toy that is out of reach?
  ¿Su hija trata de agarrar un juguete que está fuera de su alcance?

Scoring Criteria:
The child makes physical efforts to reach and recover a toy. The child may reach, lean, crawl, or roll toward the toy at any time during the assessment.

18

Imitates stirring with a spoon

Does the child imitate stirring a spoon in a cup?

Materials: two large cups and spoons

Elicit:
Model stirring a spoon in a cup. Give the child a
cup and spoon. Prompt the child to stir the spoon
in the cup.

Report:
• Does your child imitate stirring a spoon in a cup?
  ¿Su hija imita revolver una cuchara en una taza?

Scoring Criteria:
The child imitates stirring a spoon in a cup.

19

Pushes a toy car

Does the child push a toy car?

Materials: toy cars

Elicit:
Place the toy cars within the child's reach. Model
pushing a car. If necessary, prompt the child to
push a car.

Report:
• How does your child play with toy cars?
  ¿Cómo juega su hija con carros de juguete?
• Does your child push toy cars?
  ¿Su hija empuja carros de juguete?

Scoring Criteria:
The child pushes a toy car.

❋ ❋ ❋ ❋ ❋ ❋ ❋ ❋ ❋ ❋

20   ### Plays fetching game with caregiver

Does the child pursue and return a toy to the caregiver?

Materials: a toy that rolls, such as a ball or a small push toy

Elicit:
Ask the caregiver to engage the child in play with a ball or push toy. Direct the caregiver to roll the toy a short distance away from the child and prompt the child to get it. When the child returns the toy to the caregiver, have her repeat the sequence.

Report:
• What does your child do if you roll a toy and ask her to return it to you?
¿Qué hace su hija si usted hace rodar un juguete y le pide que se lo devuelva?
• Does your child like to repeatedly chase after and return a toy to you?
¿A su hija le gusta repetir la acción de perseguir un juguete y devolverselo?

Scoring Criteria:
The child pursues and returns an object to the caregiver repeatedly.

21   ### Imitates patting a doll

Does the child imitate patting a doll?

Materials: a doll

Elicit:
Engage the child in play with a doll. Model patting the doll's stomach or back or hugging the doll. Give the doll to the child and prompt her to take a turn patting or hugging the doll.

Report:
• When you play with a doll, what actions does your child imitate?
Cuando usted juega con un muñeco, ¿qué acciones imita su hija?
• Does your child imitate your actions with a doll when you play together?
¿Su hija imita sus acciones con un muñeco cuando juegan juntos?

Scoring Criteria:
The child imitates patting or hugging a doll.

22 Shows shoes or clothing during play

Does the child identify shoes or clothing items as they are named during a playful exchange?

Elicit:
Engage the child in a playful exchange, pointing to body parts or toys and naming them. Occasionally ask the child to show basic clothing items, such as shoes, socks, pants, shirt, or a hat.

Report:
- Which clothing items can your child show you?
  ¿Qué prendas de ropa puede mostrarle su hija?
- Can your child show you clothing items when you name them?
  ¿Su hija puede mostrarle prendas de ropa cuando usted las nombra?

Scoring Criteria:
The child identifies one article of clothing upon request.

Testing Tip:
The young child most often points to clothing items on herself before she is able to identify clothing items on another person or a doll.

23 Demonstrates functional use of objects

Does the child show the functional use of objects during play?

Materials: a toy telephone, a book, a cup and a spoon, a puzzle, or a doll with clothing

Observe:
Observe the child's play with toys during the evaluation.

Elicit:
Present the toys to the child and model their functional use. Note the child's subsequent use of the toys.

Report:
- How does your child play with a toy telephone, a cup and spoon, a puzzle, or a doll?
  ¿Cómo juega su hija con un teléfono de juguete, una taza y cuchara, un rompecabezas o un muñeco?
- Does your child pretend to use objects like a telephone or a cup and a spoon?
  ¿Su hija pretende usar objetos como un teléfono o una taza y una cuchara?

Scoring Criteria:
The child shows the functional use of two or more objects. The child may put a telephone to her ear, turn the pages of a book, stir a spoon in the cup, attempt to place pieces in a puzzle, or attempt to dress a doll.

24 Shows symbolic use of objects

Does the child use one object to represent another object?

Observe:
Observe the child's use of objects during the evaluation.

Elicit:
Engage the child in free play. Using one of the toys present, demonstrate using one object to represent another object as part of play, such as using a spoon to "comb" a doll's hair. Note the child's subsequent use of the object.

Report:
• Does your child pretend one object is a different object during play?
¿Su hija pretende mientras juega que un objeto es otro objeto diferente?

Scoring Criteria:
The child uses one object to represent another object. The child may comb her hair with a spoon, pretend to write with something other than a pencil, use a block as a car, or put a shoe to her ear as a telephone.

25 Explores toys

Does the child explore toys to better understand them?

Materials: an unfamiliar toy

Observe:
Observe the child's actions with an unfamiliar toy.

Elicit:
Consult with the caregiver to select an unfamiliar toy to give the child. Observe the child's reaction to the toy.

Report:
• How does your child handle toys to learn more about them?
¿Cómo inspecciona su hija juguetes para aprender más sobre ellos?
• Does your child examine new toys to find out about them?
¿Su hija inspecciona juguetes nuevos para aprender sobre ellos?

Scoring Criteria:
The child explores and manipulates an object as she tries to better understand the object. The child may look at the object from various angles, turn the object over or try to fit objects together.

26 Plays with a toy in different ways

Does the child play with a toy in different ways?

Observe:
Observe the child's play with toys during the evaluation.

Report:
- Describe the different ways your child plays with her favorite toy.

  Describa las formas diferentes en las que su hija juega con sus juguetes preferidos.
- Does your child play with one toy in different ways?

  ¿Su hija juega con un juguete de diferentes formas?

Scoring Criteria:
The child plays with one object in different ways. The child may feed and diaper a doll, pretend to drink and pour from a cup, stack blocks and fill a cup with blocks or scribble on paper and use paper to wrap an object.

27 Plays ball with adults

Does the child play ball with an adult?

Materials: a large ball

Elicit:
Roll or gently kick the ball to the child. Prompt the child to return the ball. Continue this play sequence.

Report:
- What does your child do when you roll or throw a ball to her?

  ¿Qué hace su hija cuando le rueda o tira una pelota?
- Does your child like to play ball with you?

  ¿A su hija le gusta jugar a la pelota con usted?

Scoring Criteria:
The child plays ball cooperatively with an adult. The child may kick or roll the ball back and forth or try to play catch.

28

Places one object inside another

Does the child place one object inside of another object?

Materials: toy vehicles and small dolls, a sandbox and trucks or pails, play food and cookware, or a baby doll and a cradle

Observe:
Observe the child's play with toys during the evaluation.

Elicit:
Engage the child in play. Model placing one object inside of another object. Note the child's subsequent use of those objects.

Report:
- Which toys does your child place inside other toys?
  ¿Qué juguetes pone su hija adentro de otros juguetes?
- Does your child place one toy inside of another toy during play?
  ¿Su hija mientras juega mete un juguete adentro de otro juguete?

Scoring Criteria:
The child places one object inside another object in an appropriate manner. The child may place a "driver" in a vehicle, load sand into a dump truck, place play food in a pan, or put a doll in a cradle.

15–18 Months
Play

29 Hands a toy to an adult for assistance

Does the child hand a toy or seek assistance from an adult when she is unable to operate the toy?

Materials: wind-up toys, a See 'n Say, a battery-operated toy with a hidden switch, or a jack-in-the-box

Observe:
Observe the child's reaction to toys she is unable to operate during the evaluation.

Elicit:
Consult with the caregiver to select a toy the child is unable to operate independently. Operate the toy once to attract the child's interest. Give the toy to the child. Observe the child's reactions when she is unable to operate the toy.

Report:
• What does your child do when she can't make a toy work?
  ¿Qué hace su hija cuando no puede hacer que funcione un juguete?

Scoring Criteria:
The child hands the toy or seeks assistance when she is unable to operate the toy.

Testing Tip:
This item may be scored in conjunction with Item 21 of Interaction–Attachment on page 39.

✳ ✳ ✳ ✳ ✳ ✳ ✳ ✳ ✳ ✳

18–21 Months
Play

30 Imitates housework activities

Does the child imitate routine housework activities performed by her caregivers?

Report:
• What type of housework does your child imitate?
  ¿Que tipo de quehaceres domésticos imita su hija?
• Does your child imitate you when you do housework?
  ¿Su hija le imita cuando hace los quehaceres domésticos?

Scoring Criteria:
The child imitates housework activities. The child may attempt to dust furniture, wash dishes, sweep the floor, or throw trash away.

The Rossetti Infant-Toddler Language Scale   84   Copyright © 2006 LinguiSystems, Inc.

31 Groups objects in play

Does the child group similar objects together?

Observe:
Observe the child's play with toys during the evaluation.

Report:
• Does your child sort similar toys into groups as she plays?
¿Su hija mientras juega clasifica juguetes parecidos en grupos?
• Which toys does your child group together?
¿Qué juguetes clasifíca juntos su hija?

Scoring Criteria:
The child groups similar objects together during play. The child may group dolls and clothing, silverware and dishes, toy vehicles, toy animals, or books.

32 Uses two toys together in pretend play

Does the child use two toys together during pretend play?

Observe:
Observe the child's play with toys during the evaluation.

Report:
• Does your child use two or more toys together during her pretend play? What kinds of toys?
¿Su hija usa dos o más juguetes juntos mientras juega juegos de pretender? ¿Qué tipos de juguetes?

Scoring Criteria:
The child uses two toys together during pretend play. The child may put a vehicle in a toy garage or a toy animal in a barn, or pretend to cook with utensils and cookware.

33 Puts away toys on request

Does the child put away toys on request?

Elicit:
At the end of the evaluation, ask the child to help put away the toys.

Report:
• What does your child do when you ask her to put away her toys?
¿Qué hace su hija cuando usted le pide que guarde sus juguetes?
• Does your child put away her toys when asked?
¿Su hija guarda los juguetes cuando le pide?

Scoring Criteria:
The child puts away her toys with minimal prompting.

Testing Tip:
When administering this item, ask any siblings playing with the child to help put away the toys.

34 Attempts to repair broken toys

Does the child attempt to repair broken toys?

Materials: a toy vehicle with a tire removed, a doll with one eye glued shut or a dollhouse with a door removed

Elicit:
Engage the child in play. Find and identify a toy as broken. Present all parts of a broken toy to the child and ask her to fix it. Observe the child's reactions.

Report:
• What does your child do when she finds a broken toy?
¿Qué hace su hija cuando encuentra un juguete roto?
• Does your child try to fix broken toys?
¿Su hija trata de arreglar juguetes rotos?

Scoring Criteria:
The child attempts to fix a broken object. The child may push broken pieces together, stack broken pieces or place the pieces on a table in a manner that represents a "fixed" object.

35 Stacks and assembles toys and objects

Does the child stack and assemble play objects?

Materials: blocks or 3- to 4-piece puzzles

Observe:
Observe the child's play with toys during the evaluation.

Elicit:
Engage the child in play with blocks or a puzzle. If necessary, prompt the child to play with the toys. Observe the child's subsequent play with the toys.

Report:
• How does your child play with blocks and puzzles?
  ¿Cómo juega su hija con bloques y rompecabezas?
• Does your child stack blocks or put puzzles together?
  ¿Su hija apila bloques o une rompecabezas?

Scoring Criteria:
The child attempts to stack blocks or put a puzzle together.

Testing Tip:
Use wooden blocks for stacking activities. The slick surface of small plastic blocks often makes stacking difficult.

✳ ✳ ✳ ✳ ✳ ✳ ✳ ✳ ✳ ✳

36 Performs many related activities during play

Does the child perform many activities with the same toys during a play sequence?

Materials: dolls, doll clothing, dollhouse furniture, play food, and play cookware

Observe:
Observe the child's play during the evaluation.

Report:
• Does your child play in a variety of ways with the same toys during one play period?
  ¿Su hija juega de diferentes formas con los mismos juguetes durante un periodo de juego?
• Describe what your child does with the toys during the play period.
  Describa que hace su hija con los juguetes durante un periodo de juego.

Scoring Criteria:
The child performs many activities during an extended play sequence. The child may cook play food, feed dolls, wash play dishes, and put the dolls to bed.

Testing Tip:
This item may be scored in conjunction with Item 43 of Play on page 91.

37 Chooses toys selectively

Does the child show selectivity in her choice of toys?

Materials: a box of toys

Observe:
Observe the child as she enters any area containing a variety of toys.

Elicit:
Present the child with a box full of toys. Observe the child's reaction as she chooses toys.

Report:
- How does your child show that she prefers some toys more than other toys?
  ¿Cómo demuestra su hija que prefiere algunos juguetes más que otros?
- Does your child prefer some toys more than other toys?
  ¿Su hija prefiere algunos juguetes más que otros?

Scoring Criteria:
The child sorts through toys to select a specific toy.

Testing Tip:
This play behavior often spontaneously occurs when the child arrives at the testing center and sees the toys in the reception area.

38 Uses most toys appropriately

Does the child use most toys appropriately?

Observe:
Observe the child's spontaneous use of toys during the evaluation.

Report:
- Does your child use most of her toys appropriately?
  ¿Su hija usa la mayoría de sus juguetes apropiadamente?
- Does your child use any toys in an unusual manner? What does she do?
  ¿Su hija usa algunos juguetes de una manera fuera de lo común? ¿Qué hace?

Scoring Criteria:
The child plays with toys in a purposeful and meaningful manner. The child does not mouth toys or show other forms of immature or inappropriate play with toys.

39 Demonstrates parallel play with other children

Does the child play near other children but with minimal interaction with
those children?

Observe:
Observe the child when she is with other children
in a free-play setting.

Report:
• Describe how your child plays when she is with
other children.
Describa cómo juega su hija cuando está con
otros niños.
• Does your child play alongside other children
more than directly with them?
¿Su hija juega al lado de otros niños más que
directamente con ellos?

Scoring Criteria:
The child plays near other children but has minimal
interaction with those children. The child does not
initiate shared play routines.

40 Talks and verbalizes more in play around other children

Does the child show an increase in the amount she talks when she plays
with children?

Report:
• Have you noticed an increase in how much your
child talks when she plays near other children?
¿Ha notado un aumento en la cantidad que habla
su hija cuando juega cerca de otros niños?

Scoring Criteria:
The caregiver reports the child talks more frequently
during play with other children.

41 Shares toys with other children

Does the child share toys with other children during play activities?

Observe:
Observe the child at play with other children.

Report:
- How often or how easily does your child share toys with other children?
  ¿Qué tan amenudo o qué tan fácil comparte su hija juguetes con otros niños?
- Does your child share toys with other children during play?
  ¿Su hija comparte juguetes con otros niños mientras juega?

Scoring Criteria:
The child shares toys with other children during play at times. An adult may need to prompt the child to share.

❋ ❋ ❋ ❋ ❋ ❋ ❋ ❋ ❋ ❋

30–33 Months
Play

42 Performs longer sequences of play activities

Does the child perform longer sequences of play activities?

Observe:
Observe the child's spontaneous play during the evaluation.

Report:
- When your child is playing, does she do one thing after another using the same group of toys? Cuando su hija está jugando, ¿hace una cosa tras otra usando el mismo grupo de juguetes?

Scoring Criteria:
The child chains together longer sequences of activities. The child may scribble, color, "write" her name, and display her artwork. She may retrieve a play barn from a toy box, arrange objects and animals to create a farm and act out farming sequences.

Testing Tips:
Include toys that encourage play sequences in a free-play area. These toys may include a barn and animals, a dollhouse and dolls, a garage and toy vehicles, and housekeeping utensils and appliances.

43   Acts out familiar routines

Does the child act out familiar parts of her daily routine?

Materials: toy telephones, play cookware, house-keeping items, or a mirror and grooming items

Observe:
Observe the child's spontaneous play during the evaluation.

Elicit:
Engage the child in play with housekeeping and grooming toys. Observe the child's use of objects typically associated with daily routines.

Report:
• Which parts of your child's daily routine does she act out during play?
  ¿Qué partes de su rutina diaria pretende su hija mientras juega?
• Does your child act out parts of her daily routine during play?
  ¿Su hija pretende partes de su rutina diaria mientras juega?

Scoring Criteria:
The child acts out familiar behaviors that are part of her normal routine. The child may attempt to set the table, fold clothes, brush her teeth, or wash dishes.

Testing Tip:
This item may be scored in conjunction with Item 36 of Play on page 87.

44   Pretends to perform the caregiver's routines

Does the child act out less familiar parts of the caregiver's daily routine?

Observe:
Observe the child's spontaneous play during the evaluation.

Report:
• Which parts of your daily routine does your child act out during play?
  ¿Qué partes de su rutina diaria pretende su hija mientras juega?
• Does your child act out parts of your daily routine?
  ¿Su hija pretende partes de su rutina diaria?

Scoring Criteria:
The child acts out less familiar behaviors that are part of the caregiver's daily routine. The child may try to use the telephone, "read" a newspaper, put on makeup or lock and unlock a door with keys.

※ ※ ※ ※ ※ ※ ※ ※ ※ ※

45 Acts out a new ending to a familiar routine

Does the child add a new ending to a familiar routine she acts out during play?

Observe:
Observe the child's spontaneous play during the evaluation.

Report:
• Does your child change the usual ending to routine activities she acts out during play?
¿Su hija cambia los finales usuales de actividades rutinarias que ella pretende mientras juega?

Scoring Criteria:
The child acts out a new ending to a familiar daily routine during play. The child may spill all the food prepared for dinner, or have a doll play the child's role by putting the mother or father doll to bed.

46 Uses a doll as a playmate

Does the child play with a doll as if it were a playmate?

Materials: a doll

Observe:
Observe the child's spontaneous play with dolls during the evaluation.

Report:
• Does your child act as if a doll is a real playmate at times?
¿Su hija pretende aveces que su muñeco es un compañero de juego verdadero?

Scoring Criteria:
The child plays with a doll or prop as if it were a playmate at times. The child directs and positions a doll in its role during play. The child may converse with the doll, pretend to share a snack with the doll or bring toys to the doll.

47 Uses one object to represent many objects

Does the child use one object to represent different objects at different times?

Observe:
Observe the child's spontaneous play during the evaluation.

Report:
• Does your child use one object as if it were a different object at different times?
¿Su hija usa un objeto en diferentes ocasiones como si fuera un objeto diferente?

Scoring Criteria:
The child uses one object to represent different objects at different times. The child may "shoot" with a stick and then later pretend it is a musical instrument, use a scarf as a blanket or a tablecloth or pretend a couch is a school bus or a boat.

1

Quiets to a familiar voice

Does the child quiet when he is fussing in response to a familiar voice?

Observe:
If the child cries or fusses during the evaluation, note his response when the caregiver tries to comfort him by talking to him.

Report:
- What happens when your child is fussing and you begin to talk to him?
  ¿Qué pasa cuando su hijo está fastidiado y usted empieza a hablar con él?
- If your child is fussing, does he quiet when he hears your voice?
  Si su hijo está fastidiado, ¿se calma cuando escucha su voz?

Scoring Criteria:
The child quiets when he is fussing and hears a familiar voice.

Testing Tip:
This item may be scored in conjunction with Item 10 of Interaction–Attachment on page 34 and Item 11 of Language Comprehension on page 98.

2

Moves in response to a voice

Does the child move in response to a pleasant voice?

Observe:
Note the child's activity level when he is calm and alone. Note any changes in the child's activity level when an adult talks to him in a pleasant manner.

Elicit:
When the child is calm, ask the caregiver to talk to him in a pleasant manner. Observe the child's response.

Report:
- What happens when your child is calm and you begin to talk to him in a pleasant manner?
  ¿Qué pasa cuando su hijo está calmado y usted empieza a hablarle de una manera agradable?
- Does your child become more active when you talk to him in a friendly manner?
  ¿Su hijo se vuelve más activo cuando usted le habla de una manera amigable?

Scoring Criteria:
The child becomes active when he hears a pleasant voice. He may move his limbs, head or eyes in response to the voice.

Language Comprehension

3

Shows awareness of a speaker

Does the child seem aware when someone is talking to him?

Observe:
Observe the child's reactions when an adult talks to him during the evaluation.

Elicit:
Talk to the child in a pleasant manner. Note his response.

Report:
- How can you tell when your child knows you're talking to him?
  ¿Cómo puede decir cuando su hijo sabe que usted está hablando con él?
- Does your child seem to know when you are talking to him?
  ¿Su hijo parece saber cuando usted le está hablando?

Scoring Criteria:
The child seems to listen to the speaker briefly. The child may establish eye contact with the speaker, smile and show a brief change in physical activity as the speaker begins to talk. Changes may include arm and leg movements, facial expressions or respiratory patterns.

4

Attends to other voices

Does the child attend to voices other than the caregiver's?

Observe:
Observe the child's reaction to adults who are nearby talking.

Elicit:
Talk to the caregiver while you are close to the child. Note the child's reactions to your voice.

Report:
- How does your child respond when unfamiliar people are talking near him?
  ¿Cómo responde su hijo cuando personas extrañas hablan cerca de él?
- Does your child pay attention to other people's voices?
  ¿Su hijo presta atención a las voces de otras personas?

Scoring Criteria:
The child attends to voices other than the caregiver's. The child may quiet, look at the speaker's face or establish eye contact with the speaker.

5 Attends to a speaker's mouth or eyes

Does the child attend to the speaker's mouth or eyes?

Observe:
Observe the child's reactions as adults talk to him at close range.

Elicit:
Talk to the child at close range. Note where the child gazes as you speak to him.

Report:
- Where does your child look when you are talking to him at close range?
  ¿Adónde mira su hijo cuando usted le está hablando de cerca?
- Does your child look at your mouth or eyes when you talk to him?
  ¿Su hijo mira a su boca o a sus ojos cuando usted habla con él?

Scoring Criteria:
The child attends to the speaker's mouth or eyes.

6 Discriminates between harsh and soothing voices

Does the child respond differently to a harsh voice and a soothing voice?

Report:
- How does your child react when someone speaks to him in a harsh voice?
  ¿Cómo reacciona su hijo cuando alguien le habla en tono de voz fuerte?
- How does your child react when someone speaks to him in a soothing voice?
  ¿Cómo reacciona su hijo cuando alguien le habla en un tono de voz calmado?
- Does your child respond differently to harsh and soothing voices?
  ¿Su hijo reacciona differente a tonos de voces fuertes o calmados?

Scoring Criteria:
The child changes affect or activity level in response to the speaker's tone of voice. The child may frown, cry or startle in response to a harsh voice. He may smile when spoken to pleasantly, widen his eyes or stop all physical activity.

Testing Tip:
It is not recommended that the examiner speak angrily in an attempt to directly elicit a response from the child. The child and caregiver may become upset. This item may be scored in conjunction with Item 2 of Interaction–Attachment on page 29, Item 13 of Language Comprehension on page 99, and Item 15 of Language Comprehension on page 100.

7

Turns head toward a voice

Does the child turn his head toward a speaker?

Observe:
Observe the child's reaction as people out of his line of vision talk to him.

Elicit:
Stand outside of the child's line of vision and speak in a friendly voice to the child. Note the child's reaction.

Report:
• What does your child do when he hears someone talking but can't see that person?
  ¿Qué hace su hijo cuando escucha a alguien hablando pero no puede ver a la persona?
• Does your child turn his head toward a person who is talking when he can't see that person?
  ¿Su hijo voltea la cabeza hacia una persona que esta hablando cuando no puede ver a la persona?

Scoring Criteria
The child turns his head toward the location of the speaker.

8

Searches for the speaker

Does the child look around in search of the speaker?

Observe:
Observe the child as adults talk nearby.

Elicit:
Talk to the caregiver while close to the child. Note the child's reactions.

Report:
• Does your child look at the faces of people to find out who's talking?
  ¿Su hijo mira a las caras de personas para encontrar quien está hablando?

Scoring Criteria:
The child scans the area and the faces of the people present in search of the person talking.

9

Responds to sounds other than voices

Does the child show an awareness of sounds other than voices?

Materials: a rattle, a bell or a noisemaker

Observe:
Observe the child's reaction to environmental sounds during the evaluation.

Elicit:
Shake the rattle or noisemaker or ring the bell. Note the child's reaction.

Report:
• Which sounds does your child respond to other than voices?
  Aparte de voces, ¿a qué sonidos responde su hijo?
• Does your child respond to sounds other than voices?
  ¿Su hijo responde a otros sonidos que no sean voces?

Scoring Criteria:
The child shows an awareness of sounds as well as voices. He may turn his head toward the source of the sound, smile or frown at the sound or search for the source of the sound.

10

Recognizes own name

Does the child recognize his name?

Elicit:
Talk to the child and periodically call his name. Note the child's reaction.

Report:
• What does your child do when you call his name?
  ¿Qué hace su hijo cuando usted lo llama por su nombre?
• Does your child recognize his name?
  ¿Su hijo reconoce el nombre de él?

Scoring Criteria:
The child responds differently to his name than to general verbalization. He may smile, brighten, or increase his activity when his name is called.

11

Stops crying when spoken to

Does the child stop crying when a person talks to him?

Observe:
If the child cries during the evaluation, observe his reaction as an adult approaches him and talks to him.

Report:
- How do you stop your child's crying?
  ¿Cómo hace para que su hijo pare de llorar?
- Can you stop your child's crying by talking to him?
  ¿Usted puede hablar con su hijo para que pare de llorar?

Scoring Criteria:
The child stops crying when a person talks to him.

Testing Tip:
This item may be scored in conjunction with Item 10 of Interaction–Attachment on page 34 and Item 1 of Language Comprehension on page 93.

12

Responds to "no" half of the time

Does the child stop half of the time when an adult says "no"?

Observe:
Observe the child's reactions if the caregiver says "no" to him several times during the evaluation.

Report:
- What does your child do when you say "no" to him?
  ¿Qué hace su hijo cuando usted le dice "no"?
- Does your child always stop what he is doing when you say "no" to him?
  ¿Su hijo siempre para lo que está haciendo cuando usted le dice "no"?

Scoring Criteria:
The child stops or withdraws about half of the time when an adult says "no."

Testing Tip:
This item may be scored in conjunction with Item 19 of Language Comprehension on page 102.

13

Discriminates between threatening and friendly voices

Does the child discriminate between a threatening and a friendly voice in a person?

Report:
- How does your child react when a person sounds angry with him compared to when a person is pleasant with him?
  ¿Cómo reacciona su hijo cuando una persona suena enojada con él comparado con cuando una persona le habla de una manera agradable?
- Does your child seem to know if a person is angry with him? If so, how?
  ¿Su hijo parece darse cuenta si una persona está enojada con él? ¿Si es así, cómo?
- Does your child smile and brighten when a person is pleasant with him?
  ¿Su hijo sonríe y se alegra cuando una persona es agradable con él?

Scoring Criteria:
The child discriminates between threatening and friendly voices. The child may look very serious or uncertain when hearing an angry voice and appear to brace himself for an unpleasant interaction. The child smiles, brightens and becomes livelier when hearing a friendly voice.

Testing Tip:
This item may be scored in conjunction with Item 2 of Interaction–Attachment on page 29, Item 6 of Language Comprehension on page 95, and Item 15 of Language Comprehension on page 100.

14

Anticipates feeding

Does the child anticipate feeding from the routines that precede feeding?

Observe:
If the child is fed during the evaluation, note his reactions as the caregiver prepares a bottle or positions him for feeding.

Report:
- What does your child do as you prepare his bottle or get ready to feed him?
  ¿Qué hace su hijo mientras usted le prepara su biberón o se alista para darle de comer?
- Does your child seem to get excited when you prepare his bottle or get ready to feed him?
  ¿Su hijo parece entusiasmarse cuando usted le prepara el biberón o se alista para darle de comer?

Scoring Criteria:
The child shows anxious anticipation during the routines that precede feeding. He becomes excited when the refrigerator is opened, when his caregiver sits with him in a rocking chair and positions him for feeding, or when the caregiver says it is time to eat.

15 Cries at an angry tone of voice

Does the child cry when he hears an angry tone of voice?

Report:
- What does your child do when he hears an angry tone of voice?
  ¿Qué hace su hijo cuando escucha un tono de voz enfadado?
- Does your child cry when he hears an angry tone of voice?
  ¿Su hijo llora cuando escucha un tono de voz enfadado?

Scoring Criteria:
The child cries when he hears an angry tone of voice from a nearby person.

Testing Tip:
This item may be scored in conjunction with Item 2 of Interaction–Attachment on page 29, Item 6 of Language Comprehension on page 95, and Item 13 of Language Comprehension on page 99.

16 Recognizes family members' names

Does the child recognize family members when they are named?

Elicit:
Bring all available family members together with the child. Say "Where's _____?" for each family member. Note the child's responses.

Report:
- What does your child do when he hears you say a family member's name?
  ¿Qué hace su hijo cuando le escucha decir el nombre de un miembro de la familia?
- Does your child look for family members when you say their names?
  ¿Su hijo busca a miembros de la familia cuando usted dice sus nombres?

Scoring Criteria:
The child recognizes the names of immediate family members. The child may look at the person named or smile and search the room for that person if he is not present.

17

Responds with gesture to "come up" or "want up?"

Does the child respond with gesture to phrases such as "come up" or "want up"?

Observe:
Observe the child's reaction if the caregiver gives him simple directions such as "come up" during the evaluation.

Elicit:
Say "come up" to the child and note his response.

Report:
• What does your child do when you say "come up" to him?
   ¿Qué hace su hijo cuando le dice "ven"?
• Does your child reach up or lean toward you when you say "come up"?
   ¿Su hijo extiende los brazos o se inclina hacia usted cuando le dice "ven"?

Scoring Criteria:
The child responds with appropriate gestures to simple phrases like "come up" when they are given with or without gestures. The child may extend his arms and lean toward the speaker when he hears "come up."

Testing Tip:
First administer this item without using gestures when you say "come up" to the child. Repeat the phrases using gestures only if the child does not respond. Presenting phrases without gestures provides information about the child's understanding of verbal language independent of his reliance on gestures.

18

Attends to music or singing

Does the child attend to music or singing?

Materials: a tape recorder and a tape of children's music, a radio or any source of music

Elicit:
Turn on the music and note the child's reaction.

Report:
• What does your child do when he hears music or singing?
   ¿Qué hace su hijo cuando escucha música o a alguien cantando?
• Does your child pay attention to music or singing?
   ¿Qué hace su hijo cuando escucha música o a alguien cantando?

Scoring Criteria:
The child attends to music or singing. He may stop all physical activity momentarily, become more active or quiet, or look for the source of the music.

19

Responds to "no" most of the time

Does the child stop most of the time when an adult says "no"?

Observe:
Observe the child's reactions if the caregiver says "no" to him several times during the evaluation.

Report:
• What does your child do when you say "no" to him?
¿Qué hace su hijo cuando usted le dice "no"?
• Does your child stop most of the time when you say "no" to him?
¿Su hijo para la mayor parte del tiempo cuando usted le dice "no"?

Scoring Criteria:
The child stops or withdraws most of the time when an adult says "no."

Testing Tip:
This item may be scored in conjunction with Item 12 of Language Comprehension on page 98.

20

Maintains attention to a speaker

Does the child maintain attention when a person speaks to him?

Observe:
Observe the child's reactions as adults speak to him during the evaluation.

Elicit:
Talk to the child pleasantly and note his reactions.

Report:
• What does your child do when people speak to him pleasantly for a while?
¿Qué hace su hijo cuando personas le hablan por un rato de una manera agradable?
• Does your child maintain his attention to people who talk to him?
¿Su hijo presta atención a personas que le hablan?

Scoring Criteria:
The child maintains his attention to a speaker for a long period of time. He may stop all physical activity, smile or maintain consistent eye contact with the speaker while listening.

21

Responds to sounds when the source is not visible

Does the child respond to environmental noises when their source is not visible?

Observe:
Observe the child's reactions to environmental sounds when their source is not visible.

Report:
- How does your child react when he hears a sound but can't see the source of the sound?
  ¿Cómo reacciona su hijo cuando escucha un sonido pero no ve de donde viene?
- Does your child respond to sounds when he can't see the source of the sound?
  ¿Su hijo responde a sonidos cuando no puede ver de donde viene el sonido?

Scoring Criteria:
The child actively responds to a new or familiar sound although he can't see its source. The child may smile or become lively when he hears the family dog bark or a sibling call from outside. He may stop moving when he hears a phone ring in another room.

22

Stops when name is called

Does the child stop what he is doing when his name is called?

Observe:
Observe the child's response if the caregiver calls his name during the evaluation.

Elicit:
Periodically call out the child's name when he is engaged in play. Note his response.

Report:
- What does your child do when you call his name?
  ¿Qué hace su hijo cuando usted lo llama por su nombre?
- Does your child stop moving momentarily when you call out his name?
  ¿Su hijo para de moverse por un momento cuando usted lo llama por su nombre?

Scoring Criteria:
The child stops what he is doing when his name is called.

Testing Tip:
This item may be scored in conjunction with Item 27 of Language Comprehension on page 106.

---

23 Attends to pictures

Does the child briefly attend to pictures as they are named?

Materials: simple books showing pictures of animals or familiar objects

Observe:
Observe the child if the caregiver looks through books with him during the evaluation.

Elicit:
Place the child in a comfortable position that allows him to look at a book as you point to and name the pictures. Note the child's reactions.

Report:
- What does your child do when you point to and name pictures for him?
  ¿Qué hace su hijo cuando usted señala y nombra dibujos para él?
- Does your child look at pictures briefly when you point to and name them?
  ¿Su hijo mira brevemente a dibujos cuando usted los señala y nombra?

Scoring Criteria:
The child attends to pictures for a brief period of time.

Testing Tip:
Choose books that have only one or two realistic pictures on a page. At this age, children often find animals, familiar objects or pictures of familiar people interesting.

---

24 Waves in response to "bye-bye"

Does the child wave when a person says "bye-bye" to him?

Elicit:
Say "bye-bye" without gesturing to the child as he leaves the room or as you leave the room. If the child does not respond, repeat the routine and wave at the child while saying "bye-bye."

Report:
- What does your child do when someone says "bye-bye" to him as he leaves?
  ¿Qué hace su hijo cuando alguien al irse le dice "adiós"?
- Does your child wave when someone says "bye-bye" to him as he leaves?
  ¿Su hijo hace señales con la mano cuando alguien al irse le dice "adiós"?

Scoring Criteria:
The child waves in response to "bye-bye" presented with or without gestures.

Testing Tip:
Monitor the amount a child relies on gestures over time as a measure of his language comprehension development.

✳ ✳ ✳ ✳ ✳ ✳ ✳ ✳ ✳ ✳

25 Attends to new words

Does the child show interest in listening to new words?

Report:
- How does your child show he is interested in learning new names for objects, people or places?
  ¿Cómo muestra su hijo que está interesado en aprender nombres nuevos de objetos, personas o lugares?
- Does your child seem interested in listening to new names for objects, people or places?
  ¿Su hijo parece interesado en escuchar nombres nuevos de objetos, personas o lugares?

Scoring Criteria:
The child shows increased interest in listening to new words. He attends to the word and the object it represents more intently and is less distracted by other sights or sounds as new objects or people are presented.

26 Gives objects upon verbal request

Does the child give familiar objects to an adult upon verbal request?

Materials: age-appropriate toys, such as a ball; plastic rings; beads; dolls or toy animals; or familiar objects, such as socks or shoes

Observe:
Observe the child's response if the caregiver asks him for an object during the evaluation.

Elicit:
Ask the caregiver to select three objects that are familiar to the child. Place the objects near the child. Without gesturing toward the object, ask the child to give you the object.

Report:
- What things can your child give you when you ask for them?
  ¿Qué cosas le puede dar su hijo cuando usted se las pide?
- Can your child give you familiar objects when you ask him?
  ¿Su hijo puede darle objetos familiares cuando usted se los pide?

Scoring Criteria:
The child gives a familiar object to an adult upon verbal request.

Testing Tip:
When the child is scheduled for an assessment away from home, encourage the caregiver to bring some of the child's favorite toys to use during the evaluation. Consult with the caregiver before you administer this item to ensure you call all objects by the same names that are used within the home.

27 Looks at person saying child's name

Does the child look at a person who says his name?

Observe:
Observe the child's response if a person calls his name during the evaluation.

Elicit:
Engage the child in play. Periodically call the child's name. Note the child's response.

Report:
- What does your child do when a person calls his name?
  ¿Qué hace su hijo cuando una persona dice su nombre?
- Does your child consistently look at you when you call his name?
  ¿Su hijo le mira de una forma consistente cuando usted dice su nombre?

Scoring Criteria:
The child consistently looks at the person who calls his name.

Testing Tip:
This item may be scored in conjunction with Item 22 of Language Comprehension on page 103.

28 Performs a routine activity upon verbal request

Does the child perform daily routine activities upon verbal request?

Report:
- Which of your child's daily activities is he able to perform when you tell him?
  ¿Cuáles actividades diarias puede hacer su hijo cuando usted le pide?
- Does your child perform activities that are part of his daily routine when you ask him?
  Cuando usted le pide, ¿su hijo hace actividades que son parte de su rutina diaria?

Scoring Criteria:
The child performs simple activities that are part of his daily routine upon verbal request. He may try to wipe his face or comb his hair when asked.

29 Looks at familiar objects and people when named

Does the child look at familiar objects and people when they are named?

Materials: age-appropriate toys, such as a ball, a rattle, plastic keys, a doll or a stuffed animal, or the child's toys and personal items provided by the caregiver

Elicit:
Ask the caregiver to select three objects that are familiar to the child. Place the objects near the child and ask him to find one of them, or ask the child to look for familiar people.

Report:
- Which objects or people does your child look at or reach for when you name them?
  ¿A qué objetos o personas mira su hijo o trata de alcanzar cuando usted los nombra?
- Does your child look at or reach for objects and people when you name them?
  ¿Su hijo mira o trata de alcanzar objetos y personas cuando usted los nombra?

Scoring Criteria:
The child consistently looks at familiar objects and people when they are named.

30 Attends to objects mentioned during conversation

Does the child attend to objects mentioned during conversation?

Observe:
Observe the child's reactions as the names of objects are mentioned during conversation.

Elicit:
Talk to the child about the toys and objects around him. Note where he looks as you mention the names of objects.

Report:
- What does your child do when you mention toys or objects as you talk to him?
  ¿Qué hace su hijo cuando usted menciona juguetes u objetos mientras habla con él?
- Does your child look at the toys or objects you mention as you are talking to him?
  ¿Su hijo mira los juguetes u objetos que usted menciona mientras usted está hablando con él?

Scoring Criteria:
The child looks at toys or objects mentioned as part of conversation.

31 Follows simple commands occasionally

Does the child occasionally follow simple verbal commands?

Materials: age-appropriate toys, such as a ball, a rattle, plastic keys, a doll, a stuffed animal, or a busy box

Observe:
Observe the child's reaction to commands the caregiver gives him during the evaluation.

Elicit:
Engage the child in play. Periodically give the child verbal commands about the toys, such as "Hug the baby." Do not use gestures. Note the child's responses.

Report:
- What does your child do when you ask him to follow simple directions with his toys?
  ¿Qué hace su hijo cuando le pide que siga direcciones simples con sus juguetes?
- Does your child occasionally follow simple directions you give him?
  ¿Su hijo sigue algunas veces direcciones simples que usted le da?

Scoring Criteria:
The child inconsistently follows simple commands presented without gesture. The child may hand an object to an adult or act upon a toy in a specific way requested.

32 Understands simple questions

Does the child understand simple questions asked about his daily routines?

Report:
- What questions can you ask your child during your daily routines that he understands?
  ¿Qué preguntas puede preguntarle a su hijo durante rutinas diarias que él conoce?
- Does your child understand the simple questions you ask him as part of your daily routine?
  ¿Su hijo entiende preguntas simples que usted le pregunta como parte de su rutina diaria?

Scoring Criteria:
The child shows that he understands at least one question about his daily routine through his actions. He may move to the refrigerator when asked if he wants a drink, go to his high chair when asked if he is ready for lunch or try to get in a chair when asked if he wants to look at a book.

33 Gestures in response to verbal requests

Does the child gesture to show his understanding of verbal requests?

Observe:
Observe the child's responses to requests the caregiver gives him during the evaluation.

Elicit:
Ask the caregiver to describe situations when the child gestures in response to a verbal request. Present similar requests to the child and note his responses.

Report:
- When does your child respond to your requests with gestures?
  ¿Cuándo responde su hijo con gestos a lo que usted le pide?
- Does your child respond to your requests with gestures at times?
  ¿Su hijo algunas veces responde con gestos a lo que usted le pide?

Scoring Criteria:
The child responds with gestures to verbal requests given without gestures. The child may blow a kiss upon request, clap his hands when asked to play "Patty-cake," cover his face when asked "Where's baby?" or shake his head "no" in response to a request.

34 Verbalizes or vocalizes in response to verbal requests

Does the child verbalize or vocalize in response to verbal requests?

Observe:
Observe the child's responses to requests the caregiver gives him during the evaluation.

Elicit:
Ask the caregiver to describe situations when the child vocalizes or verbalizes in response to a verbal request. Present similar requests to the child and note his responses.

Report:
- When does your child respond to your requests by saying a word or making sounds?
  ¿Cuándo responde su hijo a lo que usted le pide con palabras o haciendo sonidos?
- Does your child respond to your requests by saying a word or making sounds at times?
  ¿Su hijo responde algunas veces a lo que usted le pide diciendo una palabra o haciendo sonidos?

Scoring Criteria:
The child verbalizes or vocalizes in response to a verbal request given without gestures. The child may say "no" in response to a request or may make animal sounds when prompted to by an adult.

35 Participates in speech-routine games

Does the child participate in repetitive games in which an adult verbalizes and the child responds?

Elicit:
Ask the caregiver to describe speech-routine games she plays with her child. Attempt to engage the child in these games.

Report:
• What games can you play with your child in which you say something and your child verbalizes something back in response?
¿Qué juegos puede jugar con su hijo en los que usted dice algo y él le responde diciendo algo?
• Does your child play games in which you say something and he responds to what you say?
¿Su hijo juega juegos en los que usted dice algo y él responde a lo que usted dice?

Scoring Criteria:
The child participates in speech-routine games. The child may point to body parts or to family members as they are named by an adult. The child may clap in response to "Patty-cake" or cover his face when he hears "peek-a-boo."

Testing Tip:
This item may be scored in conjunction with Item 14 of Play on page 76.

36 Identifies two body parts on self

Does the child identify two of his body parts?

Elicit:
Ask the child to point to his body parts as you name them.

Report:
• Which of his body parts can your child show you when you name them?
¿Qué partes del cuerpo le puede mostrar su hijo cuando usted las nombra?
• Can your child identify two or more of his body parts when you name them?
¿Su hijo puede identificar dos o más partes del cuerpo cuando usted las nombra?

Scoring Criteria:
The child identifies two of his body parts.

Testing Tip:
Eyes, nose, mouth, hair, tummy, and ears are often the most familiar body parts for the young child.

37 Follows one-step commands during play

Does the child respond appropriately to one-step commands given without gestures during play?

Materials: age-appropriate toys, such as simple puzzles, stacking rings, blocks, beads, a busy box, or dolls

Observe:
Observe the child's responses to verbal commands given without gestures by the caregiver during the evaluation.

Elicit:
Engage the child in play with toys. Ask the child to follow simple commands with the toys during play. When the child is playing with stacking rings, you might hand him a ring and say "Put it on." As an alternative, you might say "Push it down" when he's playing with a busy box. Note the child's responses.

Report:
• What does your child do when you give him a short command without gesturing?
   ¿Qué hace su hijo cuando le da una instrucción simple sin usar gestos?
• Does your child follow simple commands you give him without gesturing?
   ¿Su hijo sigue instrucciones simples que usted le da sin usar gestos?

Scoring Criteria:
The child responds appropriately to one-step commands given without gestures during play.

38

Responds to requests to say words

Does the child say specific words upon request?

Observe:

Observe the child's response if the caregiver asks him to say words during the evaluation.

Elicit:

Ask the caregiver to select objects or toys from those available at the testing site with names that are part of the child's vocabulary. Engage the child in play with the objects or toys. Ask the child to say these words during play.

Report:

- What words can your child say when you ask him to say them?

  ¿Qué palabras puede decir su hijo cuando usted le pide que las diga?

- Does your child say words when you ask him to say them?

  ¿Su hijo dice palabras cuando usted le pide que las diga?

Scoring Criteria:

The child says at least two words upon request.

39

Maintains attention to pictures

Does the child maintain attention to pictures as they are named for a long period of time?

Materials: children's books, pictures of familiar objects or photographs of familiar people

Observe:
Observe the child if the caregiver looks through books with him during the evaluation.

Elicit:
Place the child in a comfortable position that allows him to look at pictures as you or the caregiver point to and name them. Note the amount of time the child attends to each page and the amount of time the child maintains interest in the overall task.

Report:
- What does your child do when you point to and name pictures for him for several minutes?
  ¿Qué hace su hijo cuando usted le muestra y nombra dibujos por algunos minutos?
- Will your child look at pictures as you point to them and name them for several minutes?
  ¿Su hijo mira dibujos por algunos minutos cuando usted se las muestra y nombra?

Scoring Criteria:
The child looks at pictures for several minutes. He attends to each page completely and is not easily distracted by other toys, people or sounds during this time.

40

Enjoys rhymes and finger plays

Does the child enjoy rhymes and finger plays presented by an adult?

Materials: a book of rhymes or finger plays

Elicit:
Present simple rhymes and finger plays to the child, such as "The Eensy Weensy Spider" or "Where Is Thumbkin." Note his reactions.

Report:
- What does your child do when you perform rhymes and finger plays for him?
  ¿Qué hace su hijo cuando usted le dice rimas y hace juegos con las manos?
- Does your child enjoy when you perform rhymes and finger plays for him?
  ¿A su hijo le gusta cuando usted le dice rimas y hace juegos con las manos?

Scoring Criteria:
The child smiles, laughs, vocalizes, tries to participate, or shows other signs of pleasure when he hears rhymes and finger plays.

Responds to "give me" command

Does the child respond to the command "give me" when it is presented without gestures?

Materials: age-appropriate toys, such as simple puzzles, stacking rings, blocks, beads, a busy box, and dolls

Observe:
Observe the child's response if the caregiver asks the child to give him an object during the evaluation.

Elicit:
Engage the child in play. Ask the child to give you the toy he is holding. Do not gesture when giving the command.

Report:
• What does your child do when you ask him to give you an object without holding out your hand or pointing to the object?
¿Qué hace su hijo cuando usted sin darle la mano o indicar con el dedo le pide que le de un objeto?
• Does your child respond when you ask him to give you an object without holding out your hand or pointing to the object?
¿Su hijo responde cuando usted le pide que le de un objeto sin darle la mano o indicar al objeto?

Scoring Criteria:
The child gives the requested object to the caregiver or examiner in response to the command.

Testing Tip:
If the child appears unwilling to give up toys, select one or two objects of lesser interest to the child, mix them with the toys, and attempt the item again asking for the least desired object.

42

Points to two action words in pictures

Does the child point to two action pictures when they are named?

Materials: ten pictures of common actions

Elicit:
Give the pictures to the caregiver and ask her to select three that are familiar to the child. Present the pictures to the child and ask him to show you each of the actions as you name them.

Report:
- Which action pictures can your child point to as you name them?
  ¿Qué dibujos de acciones puede mostrar su hijo mientras usted los nombra?
- Is your child able to point to action pictures as you name them?
  ¿Su hijo puede mostrar dibujos de acciones mientras usted los nombra?

Scoring Criteria:
The child points to two action pictures when they are named.

43

Understands some prepositions

Does the child show some understanding of simple prepositions, such as *in*, *on* or *under*?

Materials: blocks and a cup, stacking rings, toy vehicles or small dolls, and a box

Observe:
Observe the child's response if the caregiver asks him to follow commands involving simple prepositions during the evaluation.

Elicit:
Engage the child in play. Ask the child to place toys in, on or under other objects as part of the play.

Report:
- What does your child do when you ask him to put an object in, on or under other objects?
  ¿Qué hace su hijo cuando le pide que ponga un objeto adentro, encima o abajo de otros objetos?
- Does your child correctly follow directions to put objects in, on or under other objects?
  ¿Su hijo sigue correctamente instrucciones para poner objetos adentro, encima o abajo de otros objetos?

Scoring Criteria:
The child shows some understanding of simple prepositions. He may occasionally place objects in, on or under other objects upon request.

44

Understands new words

Does the child understand new words on a regular basis?

Report:
- How often does your child show that he understands a new word?
  ¿Qué tan amenudo muestra su hijo que él entiende una palabra nueva?
- How many new words does your child seem to understand each week?
  ¿Su hijo puede mostrar sus ojos, nariz, oídos, manos, pies, o pelo cuando usted los nombra?

Scoring Criteria:
The caregiver reports the child shows that he understands new words each week. The child may look at, reach for or point toward more objects when they are named, or he may follow more directions.

45

Identifies three body parts on self or a doll

Does the child identify three body parts on himself or a doll?

Materials: a doll

Elicit:
Ask the child to point to body parts, such as eyes, nose, feet, or tummy on himself or a doll.

Report:
- Which body parts can your child point to as you name them?
  ¿Qué partes del cuerpo puede mostrar su hijo cuando usted las nombra?
- Can your child point to his eyes, nose, ears, hands, feet, or hair when you name them?
  ¿Su hijo puede mostrar sus ojos, nariz, oídos, manos, pies, o pelo cuando usted los nombra?

Scoring Criteria:
The child identifies three body parts on himself or a doll.

Testing Tip:
Use a realistic-looking doll when assessing body part identification with young children. This item may be scored with Item 46 of Language Comprehension on page 117.

46

Identifies six body parts or clothing items on a doll

Does the child identify six body parts or clothing items on a doll?

Materials: a doll with clothing

Elicit:
Ask the child to point to body parts or clothing items on a doll.

Report:
- Which body parts or clothing items can your child point to on a doll as you name them?
  ¿Qué partes del cuerpo o artículos de ropa puede mostrar su hijo en un muñeco cuando usted los nombra?
- Can your child point to at least six body parts or clothing items on a doll when you name them?
  ¿Su hijo puede mostrar por lo menos seis partes del cuerpo o artículos de ropa en un muñeco cuando usted los nombra?

Scoring Criteria:
The child identifies six body parts or clothing items on a doll.

Testing Tip:
This item may be scored in conjunction with Item 45 of Language Comprehension on page 116.

47

Finds familiar objects not in sight

Does the child find familiar objects that are not in sight upon verbal request?

Materials: objects that belong to the child or caregiver, such as a coat, a purse, keys, a diaper bag, or a toy

Elicit:
Ask the caregiver to select an object familiar to the child. Leave this object in open view in a room as the family moves to an adjacent room. Have the caregiver ask the child to get the object. As an alternative, have the caregiver ask the child to get a familiar object that is in her purse or diaper bag.

Report:
- What happens when you ask your child to get a familiar object from another room or from your purse?
  ¿Qué pasa cuando le pide a su hijo que le traiga un objeto familiar de otra habitación o de su bolsa?
- Can your child find a familiar object in another room or from your purse when you ask for it?
  Cuando usted le pide un objeto familiar, ¿su hijo lo puede encontrar en otra habitación o en su bolsa?

Scoring Criteria:
Upon verbal request, the child finds familiar objects that are not in sight.

48

Completes two requests with one object

Does the child carry out two consecutive requests with one object?

Observe:
Observe the child's response if the caregiver asks him to follow two consecutive requests with one object during the evaluation.

Elicit:
Ask the child to carry out two consecutive requests with one object. Present both commands as one sentence. Do not gesture while giving the commands. You may ask the child to wipe his nose with a tissue and then throw it away, or to cook play food and put it on a plate.

Report:
• Can your child follow two directions in a row with one object?
   ¿Su hijo puede seguir dos instrucciones seguidas con un objeto?
• Do you need to gesture to help your child understand these directions?
   ¿Necesita hacer gestos para ayudarle a su hijo a entender estas instrucciones?

Scoring Criteria:
The child carries out two consecutive requests with one object. The child's performance is not dependent on the speaker's use of gestures.

Testing Tip:
Ask the child to follow commands with objects that have a natural sequence of events associated with them.

49

Chooses two familiar objects upon request

Does the child select two familiar objects upon request?

Materials: common objects, such as a ball, a cup, a spoon, a bottle, a block, or a toy car

Elicit:
Ask the caregiver to select three objects that are familiar to the child. Present the objects to the child and ask him to identify each object as it is named.

Report:
• Which objects can your child pick from a group of objects when you name them?
   ¿Qué objetos puede escoger su hijo de un grupo de objetos cuando usted los nombra?
• Does your child correctly choose an object you name from a group of objects?
   ¿Su hijo escoge apropiadamente un objeto que usted nombra de un grupo de objetos?

Scoring Criteria:
The child correctly selects two of the three objects when they are named.

Testing Tip:
Don't look at the test objects as you name them. The child may respond to an object because of where you look rather than because of what you say.

50

Identifies objects by category

Does the child identify objects by category?

Materials: familiar groups of objects, such as play animals, silverware, balls, dishes, doll clothing, or cars

Elicit:
Ask the caregiver which five categories of objects are most familiar to the child. Put one item from each of these five groups aside. Place the five groups of objects in front of the child. Give the child one of the items put aside and ask him where the others like it are.

Report:
- Name five categories your child knows.
  Nombre cinco categorías que su hijo sabe.
- Does your child group similar objects together in play, such as putting a spoon with a pile of silverware or a toy pig with a group of animals?
  ¿Su hijo pone objetos similares juntos cuando juega, por ejemplo, poner una cuchara en un grupo de cubiertos o un cochino de juguete en un grupo de animales?

Scoring Criteria:
The child places three objects in their correct groups.

51

Understands 50 words

Does the child understand 50 words?

Report:
- How many different words does your child understand?
  ¿Cuántas palabras diferentes entiende su hijo?
- Does your child understand at least 50 different words?
  ¿Su hijo entiende por lo menos 50 palabras diferentes?

Scoring Criteria:
The caregiver reports the child understands at least 50 words. The child may point to, reach for or look at people and objects as they are named, or he may follow action commands to demonstrate his understanding of words.

Testing Tip:
Use the word list on pages 21 or 22 or on the Parent Questionnaire to help complete this item by report.

52 Identifies four body parts and clothing items on self

Does the child identify four body parts and clothing items on himself?

Elicit:
Ask the child to point to body parts or clothing items on himself as they are named.

Report:
- Which body parts or clothing items can your child point to on himself when you name them?
  ¿Qué partes del cuerpo o artículos de ropa puede mostrar su hijo en sí mismo cuando usted los nombra?
- Can your child point to four body parts or clothing items on himself when you name them?
  ¿Su hijo puede mostrar cuatro partes del cuerpo o artículos de ropa en sí mismo cuando usted los nombra?

Scoring Criteria:
The child identifies four body parts or clothing items on himself.

53 Understands the commands "sit down" and "come here"

Does the child understand the commands "sit down" and "come here" when they are presented without gestures?

Elicit:
Ask the child to "sit down" and "come here" at appropriate times during the evaluation. Do not gesture when presenting the commands.

Report:
- Does your child respond to the commands "sit down" and "come here" when you say them without using gestures?
  ¿Su hijo responde cuando usted sin usar gestos le dice "siéntate" y "ven acá"?

Scoring Criteria:
The child understands the commands "sit down and "come here" when they are presented without gestures.

Testing Tip:
A child's failure to perform on this item may be the result of behavior difficulties rather than, or in addition to, language or cognitive difficulties.

54

Chooses five familiar objects upon request

Does the child identify five familiar objects upon verbal request?

Materials: common objects, such as a toy car, a doll, a shoe, a cup, a key, a book, a ball, a truck, a dollhouse, or a comb

Scoring Criteria:
The child identifies five familiar objects upon verbal request.

Elicit:
Present the objects in groups of three to the child. Ask the child to identify the objects as you name them. You might say "Show me the baby" or "Show me the key."

Report:
• Name five objects your child can identify when you name them.
  Nombre cinco objetos que su hijo puede identificar cuando usted los nombra.
• Can your child identify five objects when you name them?
  ¿Su hijo puede identificar cinco objetos cuando usted los nombra?

55

Understands the meaning of action words

Does the child understand the meaning of three action words?

Materials: a doll

Elicit:
Engage the child in play with a doll. Ask the child to perform actions with the doll, such as "Make baby sit," "Make baby walk," "Make baby drink," "Wipe baby's nose," or "Make baby sleep."

Scoring Criteria:
The child shows he understands the meanings of three action words by having the doll perform the requested actions.

Report:
• Name three action words your child understands.
  Nombre tres palabras que muestran acción (verbos como "saltar, jugar") que su hijo entiende.
• Can your child make a doll perform actions that you say?
  ¿Su hijo puede hacer que un muñeco haga acciones que usted le dice?

56   Identifies pictures when named

Does the child identify five pictures when they are named?

Materials: 15 pictures of common objects and actions

Elicit:
Give the pictures to the caregiver and ask her to select those that are familiar to the child. Present the pictures in groups of three to the child and ask him to point to each picture as you name it.

Report:
• Name five pictures your child can identify when you name them.
  Nombre cinco dibujos que su hijo puede identificar cuando usted los nombra.
• Can your child identify five pictures that you name?
  ¿Su hijo puede identificar cinco dibujos que usted nombra?

Scoring Criteria:
The child identifies five pictures when they are named.

57

Chooses one object from a group of five upon verbal request

Does the child identify one object from a group of five when it is named?

Materials: common objects, such as a toy car, a doll, a shoe, a cup, keys, a book, a ball, a toy truck, a dollhouse, or a comb

Elicit:
Present a group of five objects to the child. Ask the child to identify each object as it is named.

Report:
• Can your child identify one object that you name from a group of five objects?
  ¿Su hijo puede identificar un objeto que usted nombra de un grupo de cinco objetos?

Scoring Criteria:
The child correctly chooses one object from a field of five objects when it is named.

58

Follows novel commands

Does the child understand most novel commands given without gestures?

Materials: common objects, such as a toy car, a doll, a shoe, a cup, a key, a book, a ball, a toy truck, a dollhouse, or a comb

Elicit:
Place the objects in front of the child. Ask the child to follow four novel commands with the objects. These commands should request actions not typically associated with the particular object. You may ask the child to put the key in the cup, put the comb on the floor, hide the car in a shoe or drive the truck on the book. Do not gesture when giving the commands.

Report:
• Does your child understand new commands that are different from those he usually hears during his day?
  ¿Su hijo entiende cuando usted le pide que haga cosas diferentes que las que él escucha usualmente durante el día?
• Can you give examples of these commands?
  ¿Puede dar ejemplos de cosas diferentes que le pide?

Scoring Criteria:
The child correctly follows three of four novel commands given without gestures.

59 Follows a two-step related command

Does the child follow a two-step related command given without gestures?

Materials: age-appropriate toys, such as a ball, a doll, a washcloth, a baby bed, a toy vehicle, a dollhouse and garage, or a stuffed dog

Elicit:
Ask the child to follow a two-step related command, such as "Pick up the ball and roll it to me, "Park the car in the garage and then close the door," or "Pet the dog and then make him bark." Do not gesture when giving the command.

Report:
• Can your child follow two directions in a row that you give him without using gestures?
¿Su hijo puede seguir dos direcciones seguidas que usted le dice sin usar gestos?
• Can you provide examples?
¿Puede dar ejemplos?

Scoring Criteria:
The child follows a two-step related command given without gestures.

60 Understands new words rapidly

Does the child understand new words daily?

Report:
• How often does your child understand new words?
¿Qué tan amenudo entiende su hijo palabras nuevas?
• Does your child seem to understand more new words each day?
¿Su hijo parece entender más palabras nuevas cada día?
• Can you give examples of new words your child has learned recently?
¿Puede dar ejemplos de palabras nuevas que su hijo ha aprendido recientemente?

Scoring Criteria:
The caregiver reports the child understands an increasing number of words daily. The child shows his understanding of new words by following more complicated directions, by identifying more objects or concepts, or by spontaneously imitating the words.

61   Points to four action words in pictures

Does the child point to action pictures when they are named?

Materials: 12 pictures of common actions

Elicit:
Give the pictures to the caregiver and ask her to select six that are familiar to the child. Present the pictures to the child in groups of three and ask him to show you each of the actions as you name them.

Report:
• What actions can your child point to in pictures when you name them?
¿Qué acciones puede indicar su hijo en dibujos cuando usted las nombra?
• Is your child able to point to actions in pictures when you name them?
¿Su hijo puede indicar acciones en dibujos cuando usted las nombra?

Scoring Criteria:
The child points to four action pictures when they are named.

62   Recognizes family member names

Does the child recognize family members by their given names?

Elicit:
Ask the caregiver to list the names of all family members present during the evaluation. Ask the child to show you each family member as you say their names.

Report:
• Which family members is your child able to identify when you say their given names, such as Mary or John?
¿A qué miembros de la familia puede identificar su hijo cuando usted dice sus nombres, como María y Juan?
• At home is your child able to correctly identify family members when you say their given names, such as Mary or John?
¿En casa su hijo puede identificar correctamente a miembros de la familia cuando usted dice sus nombres, como María y Juan?

Scoring Criteria:
The child is able to correctly identify immediate family members by their given names.

63 Understands the concept of *one*

Does the child understand the concept of *one*?

Materials: blocks

Elicit:
Give the blocks to the child. Without gesturing, ask the child to give you one block.

Report:
• What does your child do when you ask him to give you one object from a group of objects?
¿Qué hace su hijo cuando usted le pide que le dé un objeto de un grupo de objetos?
• Is your child able to give you just one object from a group of objects when you ask him?
Cuando usted le pide, ¿su hijo puede darle solo un objeto de un grupo de objetos?

Scoring Criteria:
The child consistently gives one item upon request.

64 Understands size concepts

Does the child understand size concepts, such as *large* and *small* or *big* and *little*?

Materials: pairs of identical objects differing only in size, such as blocks, spoons, socks, cups, shoes, or balls

Elicit:
Present the pairs of objects to the child. Ask the child to find one of the objects using the terms *big*, *large*, *small*, or *little* as part of the command. You might say "Show me the big shoe" or "Where is the small spoon?"

Report:
• How can you tell your child knows the difference between *big* and *little*?
¿Cómo puede decir que su hijo sabe la diferencia entre "grande" y "pequeño"?
• Does your child know the difference between *big* and *little* or *large* and *small*?
¿Su hijo sabe la diferencia entre "grande" y "pequeño" o "grande" y "chiquito"?

Scoring Criteria:
The child shows understanding of size concepts, such as *big* and *little* or *large* and *small*. The child consistently selects the correct-sized object as it is named.

65

Responds to simple questions

Does the child correctly respond to simple *what*, *where* or *who* questions about objects or people immediately present?

Materials: toy telephones, play cookware and food, housekeeping items, dolls and clothing or grooming objects, or a dollhouse

Observe:
Observe the child's responses to questions the caregiver asks him about objects and people present.

Elicit:
Engage the child in free play. Ask the child simple questions related to his play and the objects or people present. You may ask "What do you eat with?" when pretending to pour cereal in a bowl, "Where do you sleep?" when playing with dolls and play furniture or "Who gives you cookies?" when the caregiver is present.

Report:
• Name some simple *what, where* or *who* questions that your child understands about nearby objects and people.
  Usando "qué, dónde" y "quién", nombre algunas preguntas simples que su hijo entiende sobre objetos y personas que estan cerca.
• Does your child correctly answer simple *what, where* or *who* questions about nearby objects and people?
  ¿Su hijo responde correctamente a preguntas simples usando "qué, dónde" y "quién" sobre objetos y personas que estan cerca?

Scoring Criteria:
The child correctly responds either verbally or nonverbally to simple questions about objects or people immediately present.

66 Identifies four objects by function

Does the child identify four objects by their functions?

Materials: familiar objects with common functions, such as a comb, a shoe, a scissors, a spoon, a chair, a cup, a tissue, or a hat

Elicit:
Place the objects in front of the child. Ask the child to identify each object as its function is described. You may ask the child to find the one we use to comb our hair, the one we cut with, the one we wear on our feet, or the one we drink with.

Report:
• Name four objects your child can identify when you tell him what you do with them.
  Nombre cuatro objetos que su hijo puede identificar cuando usted le dice lo que hace con ellos.
• Can your child identify objects when you tell him what you do with them?
  ¿Su hijo puede identificar objetos cuando usted le dice lo que hace con ellos?

Scoring Criteria:
The child identifies four objects when their functions are described.

67 Understands location phrases

Does the child understand two location phrases?

Materials: a ball

Elicit:
Ask the child to place an object in various locations. Do not gesture when giving the commands. You might ask the child to put the ball on the table, by the chair or in a box.

Report:
• Can your child follow directions to put objects on, in, by, or under other things?
  ¿Su hijo puede seguir direcciones para poner objetos encima, adentro, al lado o abajo de otras cosas?
• Describe some of the directions he can follow.
  Describa algunas de las direcciones que su hijo puede seguir.

Scoring Criteria:
The child understands two location phrases.

❋ ❋ ❋ ❋ ❋ ❋ ❋ ❋ ❋ ❋

68

Understands five common action words

Does the child understand five common action words?

Elicit:
Ask the child to follow commands containing common action words. Do not gesture when giving the commands. You might ask the child to clap his hands, open his mouth, jump up and down, close his eyes, or kick a ball.

Report:
- What kinds of action words does your child understand?
  ¿Qué palabras que muestran acción (verbos) entiende su hijo?
- Does your child understand five different action words, like *jump* or *kick*?
  ¿Su hijo entiende cinco diferentes palabras que muestran acción (verbos), como "saltar" o "patear"?

Scoring Criteria:
The child shows understanding of five action words by performing the actions upon request.

69

Follows two-step unrelated commands

Does the child understand two-step unrelated commands given without gestures?

Materials: common objects, such as a toy car, a doll, a shoe, a cup, keys, a book, a ball, a truck, a dollhouse, or a comb

Elicit:
Ask the child to follow two-step commands given without gestures. Present both commands as one sentence. You may ask the child to put the block in the cup and give you the car, or put the keys on the floor and pick up the doll.

Report:
- Can your child follow two directions in a row?
  ¿Su hijo puede seguir dos instrucciones seguidas?
- Can you give an example of directions he can follow?
  ¿Puede dar un ejemplo de instrucciones que puede seguir?

Scoring Criteria:
The child follows two-step unrelated commands given without gestures. Both commands are given as one sentence.

70   Understands the concepts of *one* and *all*

Does the child understand the concepts of *one* and *all*?

Materials: blocks, beads, or crayons, and a cup

Elicit:
Present the blocks, beads, or crayons and a cup to the child. Ask the child to put one block in the cup or all of the blocks in the cup, or ask the child to give you one block or all of the blocks.

Report:
- Can your child give you just one object from a group of objects when you ask?
  ¿Su hijo puede darle sólo un objeto de un grupo de objetos cuando usted le pide?
- Does your child understand when you ask him to give you all the objects in a group?
  ¿Su hijo entiende cuando usted le pide que le dé todos los objetos de un grupo?

Scoring Criteria:
The child consistently gives one object upon request or all objects upon request.

71   Answers *yes* and *no* questions correctly

Does the child correctly answer questions that require a "yes" or "no" response?

Observe:
Observe the child's response to *yes* and *no* questions the caregiver asks him during the evaluation.

Elicit:
Ask the child simple questions requiring a "yes" or "no" response, such as "Is this a key?" while holding a key or "Does a cup go on your head?" while holding a cup.

Report:
- What are some questions your child answers with "yes" or "no"?
  ¿Cuáles son algunas preguntas que su hijo responde con "sí" o "no"?
- Is your child able to correctly answer questions that need a "yes" or "no" response?
  ¿Su hijo puede responder correctamente preguntas que requieren una respuesta de "sí" o "no"?

Scoring Criteria:
The child correctly responds to questions that require a "yes" or "no" response. The child's responses may be verbal or nonverbal.

Testing Tip:
This item may be scored in conjunction with Item 82 of Language Expression on page 180.

✳ ✳ ✳ ✳ ✳ ✳ ✳ ✳ ✳ ✳

72

Shows interest in why and how things work

Does the child show interest in why and how things work?

Report:
- What are some questions your child asks about why or how things work?
  ¿Cuáles son algunas preguntas que su hijo hace sobre por qué o cómo funcionan diferentes cosas?
- Does your child ask you questions about why or how things work?
  ¿Su hijo le hace preguntas sobre por qué o cómo funcionan diferentes cosas?

Scoring Criteria:
The caregiver reports the child asks questions about why or how things work. The child might ask "Why does this go fast?" or "How do you make this go?"

73

Follows a three-step unrelated command

Does the child follow a three-step unrelated command given without gestures?

Materials: common objects, such as a toy car, a doll, a shoe, a cup, keys, a book, a ball, a truck, a dollhouse, or a comb

Elicit:
Ask the child to follow three unrelated commands given as one sentence. Present the commands without gestures. Insure the commands are not a logical sequence of actions. You might ask the child to put the comb in a cup, make the baby sit and drive the car on the floor.

Report:
- Can you give an example of the longest direction your child can follow?
  ¿Puede dar un ejemplo de la instrucción más larga que puede seguir su hijo?
- Can your child follow three directions in a row?
  ¿Su hijo puede seguir tres instrucciones seguidas?

Scoring Criteria:
The child follows a three-step unrelated command given without gestures.

74 Identifies parts of an object

Does the child identify two parts of an object?

Materials: a toy car, boat or airplane

Elicit:
Present the toy to the child. Ask the child to identify parts of the toy. You might ask the child to show you the wheels, doors, sails, windows, or wings on the toy.

Report:
- Which parts of a toy car, boat or airplane can your child identify?
  ¿Qué partes de un coche, barco o avión puede identificar su hijo?
- Can your child point to the parts of a toy car, boat or airplane when you name them?
  ¿Su hijo puede mostrar partes de un coche, barco o avión cuando usted las nombra?

Scoring Criteria:
The child identifies two parts of an object.

75 Responds to *wh-* questions

Does the child correctly respond to *what*, *where* and *who* questions about objects and people not present?

Observe:
Observe the child's responses to questions the caregiver asks him about objects or people not immediately present.

Elicit:
Engage the child in conversation. Ask the child simple *what*, *where* and *who* questions about objects and people not present. You might ask, "What did you eat for lunch?," "Where is your sister?" or "Who drives your car?"

Report:
- What kinds of *where*, *what* and *who* questions does your child answer correctly?
  ¿Qué tipo de preguntas como "dónde, qué" y "quién" puede responder su hijo correctamente?
- Does your child correctly answer *what*, *where* or *who* questions?
  ¿Su hijo responde correctamente a preguntas de "dónde, qué" y "quién"?

Scoring Criteria:
The child correctly responds to *what*, *where* and *who* questions about objects and people not present.

76

Follows commands with two familiar attributes

Does the child follow commands containing two familiar attributes?

Materials: sets of three matched objects varying in size and color, such as blocks, socks, pencils, or combs

Observe:
Note the child's response if the caregiver asks him to follow a command containing two attributes.

Elicit:
Review the child's performance on the size concepts *big, little*, *large*, and *small* from Item 64 on page 126 of Language Comprehension, the quantity concepts *all* and *one* from Item 70 on page 130 of Language Comprehension, and color concepts from Item 76 on page 176 of Language Expression. Identify two attributes familiar to the child. Ask the child to follow a command containing two of these familiar attributes, such as "Get the big, red block" or "Give me one, little sock."

Report:
• Does your child follow commands that have two descriptive words in them, such as "Get the big, red sock"?
  ¿Su hijo sigue instrucciones que tienen dos palabras descriptivas en ellas, como "Trae el calcetín rojo, grande"?
• Can you give an example of one of these commands he follows?
  ¿Puede dar un ejemplo de una de las instrucciones que él puede seguir?

Scoring Criteria:
The child follows commands containing familiar attributes, such as *big*, *little*, *one*, *dirty*, *old*, *new*, *orange*, or *purple*.

Page Intentionally
Left Blank

1 Vocalizes to caregiver's smile and voice

Does the child vocalize when the caregiver smiles and talks to her?

Observe:
Observe the child's response when the caregiver smiles and talks to her during the evaluation.

Elicit:
Ask the caregiver to smile and talk pleasantly to the child. Note the child's response.

Report:
• What does your child do when you smile and talk to her pleasantly?
  ¿Qué hace su hija cuando le sonríe y le habla de una manera amable?
• Does your child make sounds when you smile and talk to her for a while?
  ¿Su hija hace sonidos cuando le sonríe y le habla por un rato?

Scoring Criteria:
The child vocalizes when the caregiver smiles and talks to her.

Testing Tip:
This item may be scored in conjunction with Item 2 of Language Expression below and Item 9 of Language Expression on page 139.

2 Vocalizes two different sounds

Does the child produce two different sounds when she vocalizes spontaneously?

Observe:
Note the child's spontaneous vocalizations during the evaluation.

Report:
• Describe the sounds your child makes.
  Describa los sonidos que hace su hija.
• Does your child make at least two different sounds when she "talks" to you?
  ¿Su hija hace por lo menos dos sonidos cuando "habla" con usted?

Scoring Criteria:
The child produces two different vowel or consonant sounds during her spontaneous vocalizations.

Testing Tip:
This item may be scored in conjunction with Item 1 of Language Expression above and Item 9 of Language Expression on page 139.

Language Expression

3 Coos

Does the child coo, producing prolonged vowels in a singsong manner?

Observe:
Note the child's spontaneous vocalizations during the evaluation.

Report:
- Describe the sounds your child makes.
  Describa los sonidos que hace su hija.
- Does your child make vowel sounds like "ah" in a drawn out and singsong manner?
  ¿Su hija hace sonidos de vocales que suenan como "aaaa" de una manera alargada y como si estuviera cantando?

Scoring Criteria:
The child coos, producing prolonged vowels in a singsong manner.

Testing Tip:
This item may be scored in conjunction with Items 1 and 2 of Language Expression on page 135.

4 Vocalizes sounds other than crying or cooing

Does the child make sounds other than crying or cooing?

Observe:
Observe the child's spontaneous vocalizations during the evaluation. Note if the child makes vocalizations other than crying or cooing.

Report:
- Describe the sounds your child makes.
  Describa los sonidos que hace su hija.
- Does your child squeal, grunt or make a raspberry?
  ¿Su hija chilla, gruñe o deja entrar aire en su boca y lo deja salir haciendo que sus labios vibren o con la lengua entre los labios para que haga sonido?

Scoring Criteria:
The child vocalizes sounds other than crying and cooing. The child may squeal, grunt or make a raspberry or a Bronx cheer.

Testing Tip:
This item may be scored in conjunction with Items 1-3 of Language Expression on pages 135-136.

5 Produces a hunger cry

Does the child produce a specific hunger cry?

Report:
- Describe how you can tell what your child needs by the way she cries.
  Describa cómo puede decir lo que quiere su hija por la manera como llora.
- Does your child cry in a special way when she's hungry as compared to when she's wet, tired, hurt, or lonely?
  ¿Su hija llora de una manera especial cuando tiene hambre comparado con cuando está mojada, cansada, con dolor o se siente sola?

Scoring Criteria:
The child produces a specific hunger cry.

Testing Tip:
This item may be scored in conjunction with Item 6 of Pragmatics on page 43.

6 Repeats a syllable while crying

Does the child repeat a syllable while she is crying?

Observe:
Observe the child if she cries during the evaluation.

Report:
- Describe the way your child cries.
  Describa la manera en la que llora su hija.
- Does your child repeat a syllable like "mama" when she cries?
  ¿Su hija repite una sílaba como "mama" cuando llora?

Scoring Criteria:
The child repeats a syllable like "mama," "tata" or "dada" when she cries.

7 Vocalizes to express pleasure

Does the child vocalize to express pleasure?

Observe:
Note the child's vocalizations during pleasurable activities that occur during the evaluation, such as social interaction with the caregiver, feeding, holding, or rocking the child.

Report:
• Describe the sounds your child makes when she enjoys something.
  Describa los sonidos que hace su hija cuando le gusta algo.
• Can you tell if your child enjoys something by the sounds she makes?
  ¿Puede decir si a su hija le gusta algo por los sonidos que hace?

Scoring Criteria:
The child vocalizes to express pleasure. The caregiver or examiner can distinguish these vocalizations from other vocalizations.

8 Cries to get attention

Does the child cry to show she wants to be with others?

Report:
• How can you tell if your child is lonely or wants your attention?
  ¿Cómo puede decir si su hija se siente sola o quiere su atención?
• Does your child cry in a special way when she's lonely or wants your attention?
  ¿Su hija llora de una forma especial cuando se siente sola o quiere su atención?

Scoring Criteria:
The caregiver reports the child cries when she wants to be with others. The caregiver is able to distinguish between the child's cry for attention and other cries when she is wet or hungry.

Testing Tip:
This item may be scored in conjunction with Item 5 of Pragmatics on page 43.

9

Makes sounds in the back of the throat

Does the child make sounds in the back of her throat?

Observe:
Note the child's spontaneous vocalizations during the evaluation.

Report:
- Describe the sounds your child makes.
  Describa los sonidos que hace su hija.
- Does your child make sounds in the back of her throat, like /g/ or /k/?
  ¿Su hija hace sonidos en la parte de atrás de la garganta, como /g/ o /k/?

Scoring Criteria:
The child produces back sounds like /g, k/, or other sounds produced anywhere except on the lips.

Testing Tip:
The use of back sounds becomes evident as the child's tongue mobility increases. This item may be scored in conjunction with Items 1 and 2 of Language Expression on page 135.

10

Vocalizes in response to singing

Does the child vocalize in response to singing?

Elicit:
Softly sing a song to the child, such as "Rock-a-Bye Baby." Note the child's response.

Report:
- What does your child do when you sing to her?
  ¿Qué hace su hija cuando usted le canta?
- Does your child make sounds back to you when you sing to her?
  ¿Su hija le responde con sonidos cuando usted le canta?

Scoring Criteria:
The child vocalizes in response to singing.

Testing Tip:
Score this item by parent report if circumstances indicate (e.g., if it would not be fitting to sing as part of the evaluation).

11 Vocalizes feelings through intonation

Does the child use different intonation patterns to vocalize her feelings?

Observe:
Observe the child's spontaneous vocalizations during the evaluation.

Report:
- How does your child sound when she's happy or content?
  ¿Cómo suena su hija cuando está feliz o contenta?
- How does she sound when she's upset?
  ¿Cómo suena cuando está enfadada?
- How does she sound when she's lonely?
  ¿Cómo suena cuando se siente sola?
- Does your child let you know how she feels by the kind of sounds she makes?
  ¿Su hija le deja saber cómo se siente con los diferentes sonidos que hace?

Scoring Criteria:
The child vocalizes different feelings through different intonation patterns. The child may coo calmly when content, scream when upset or whine when she needs attention.

Testing Tip:
This item may be scored in conjunction with Item 6 of Pragmatics on page 43.

12 Takes turns vocalizing

Does the child take turns vocalizing with another person?

Observe:
Observe the child's response if the caregiver vocalizes to her during the evaluation.

Elicit:
Vocalize to the child in a playful manner. Pause occasionally to give the child a chance to respond. If the child vocalizes, vocalize again and then pause to see if she will respond again.

Report:
- Does your child take turns making sounds with you?
  ¿Su hija se turna haciendo sonidos con usted?
- Can you describe how your child takes turns making sounds with you?
  ¿Puede describir cómo se turna su hija haciendo sonidos con usted?

Scoring Criteria:
The child vocalizes in response to another person's vocalizations. Then the child pauses, expecting the other person to vocalize in return.

Testing Tip:
This item may be scored in conjunction with Item 8 of Pragmatics on page 44.

13 Laughs

Does the child laugh at a toy or her own activity?

Observe:
Note if the child spontaneously laughs at a toy or her own activity during the evaluation. The child's laugh should be independent of attention from another person.

Scoring Criteria:
The child laughs at a toy or her own activity. The child's laugh is not a result of another person interacting with her.

Report:
- What makes your child laugh?
  ¿Qué le hace reír a su hija?
- Does your child laugh at toys or her own activity?
  ¿Su hija se ríe de juguetes o de su propia actividad?

14 Babbles

Does the child babble, repeating the same syllable a number of times, particularly when she is alone?

Observe:
Note if the child's spontaneous vocalizations during the evaluation include babbling.

Scoring Criteria:
The child babbles, producing duplicated syllables.

Elicit:
Attempt to engage the child in a vocal exchange. Babble to the child, repeating a syllable the child spontaneously produced or is reported to produce at home.

Report:
- Describe the sounds your child makes when she is alone.
  Describa los sonidos que hace su hija cuando está sola.
- Does your child repeat the same syllable over and over, like "dadadada"?
  ¿Su hija repite la misma sílaba una y otra vez, como "dadadada"?

15 Vocalizes to express displeasure

Does the child vocalize to express displeasure?

Observe:
Note the child's vocalizations if she appears unhappy at times during the evaluation. The child may become unhappy if she is unable to reach a desired toy, if she wants attention or if she's hungry.

Report:
• Describe the sounds your child makes when she's unhappy.
  Describa los sonidos que hace su hija cuando está infeliz.
• Can you tell if your child is unhappy by the sounds she makes?
  ¿Puede decir si su hija está infeliz por los sonidos que hace?

Scoring Criteria:
The child vocalizes to express displeasure. The caregiver or examiner can distinguish these vocalizations from other vocalizations.

16 Stops babbling when another person vocalizes

Does the child stop babbling when another person vocalizes to her?

Observe:
Observe the child's vocal interactions with the caregiver during the evaluation.

Elicit:
Vocalize to the child when she begins to babble and note her response.

Report:
• What does your child do when you begin to make sounds to her while she is babbling?
  ¿Qué hace su hija cuando usted empieza a hacerle sonidos mientras ella balbucea?
• Does your child stop babbling when you begin to make sounds to her?
  ¿Su hija balbucea cuando usted empieza a hacerle sonidos?

Scoring Criteria:
The child stops babbling when another person vocalizes to her.

Testing Tip:
Ask the caregiver to engage the child in sound games similar to those played within the home to encourage the quiet child to begin babbling.

17 Initiates "talking"

Does the child initiate "talking" with another person?

Observe:
Observe the child's vocal interactions with others during the evaluation.

Scoring Criteria:
The child initiates "talking" with another person.

Report:
• Does your child start "talking" to you at times rather than waiting for you to talk first?
¿Su hija le empieza a "hablar" algunas veces en vez de esperar a que usted le hable primera?

18 Demonstrates sound play when alone or with others

Does the child play with sounds and noises when she is alone and when she is with others?

Observe:
Observe the child's spontaneous vocalizations during the evaluation.

Scoring Criteria:
The child babbles, coos or produces other vocalizations when she is alone and when she is with others.

Elicit:
Attempt to engage the child in sound play by imitating the child's sounds back to her.

Report:
• When does your child play with sounds and noises?
¿Cuándo juega su hija con sonidos y ruidos?
• Does your child play with sounds and noises when she is alone and when she is with other people?
¿Su hija juega con sonidos y ruidos cuando está sola y cuando está con otras personas?

19 Whines with a manipulative purpose

Does the child whine with a manipulative purpose?

Observe:
Observe the child's vocal interactions with others during the evaluation.

Report:
• Does your child whine?
  ¿Su hija se queja?
• Why does your child whine?
  ¿Por qué se queja su hija?
• Does your child whine because she wants something or wants you to do something for her?
  ¿Su hija se queja porque quiere algo o quiere que usted haga algo para ella?

Scoring Criteria:
The caregiver reports the child whines for a manipulative purpose. The child may whine to get the caregiver to attend to her or to obtain a desired toy or object.

20 Attempts to interact with an adult

Does the child attempt to interact with an adult?

Observe:
Observe the child's interactions with others during the evaluation.

Report:
• How does your child let you know she wants to play or "talk" with you?
  ¿Cómo le deja saber su hija que quiere jugar o "hablar" con usted?
• Does your child do things to let you know she wants to play or "talk" with you?
  ¿Su hija hace cosas para dejarle saber que quiere jugar o "hablar" con usted?

Scoring Criteria:
The child actively attempts to interact with an adult. The child may search the adult's face to establish eye contact and then smile, whine or vocalize to elicit a response.

21

Interrupts another person's vocalizations

Does the child vocalize to interrupt another person's vocalizations?

Observe:
Observe the child's vocal interaction with others during the evaluation. Note if she interrupts another person.

Elicit:
Attempt to have a vocal exchange with the child. Talk, babble, coo, or produce other vocalizations to the child, or imitate the child's vocalizations. Note when the child vocalizes in return.

Report:
• Does your child interrupt you by making sounds when you are talking or making sounds to her?
¿Su hija le interrumpe haciendo sonidos cuando usted le habla o hace sonidos con ella?

Scoring Criteria:
The child vocalizes to interrupt another person's vocalizing.

22 Vocalizes four different syllables

Does the child vocalize four different syllables?

Observe:
Observe the child's spontaneous vocalizations during the evaluation. Note the different syllables she uses.

Elicit:
Attempt to have a vocal exchange with the child. Talk, babble, coo, or produce other vocalizations to the child, or imitate the child's vocalizations. Make a list of the sounds the child produces.

Report:
• Describe the different sounds your child makes.
  Describa los diferentes sonidos que hace su hija.
• Does your child use at least four different sounds, like "ma, da" or "ga," when she vocalizes?
  ¿Su hija usa por lo menos cuatro sonidos diferentes, como "ma, da" o "ga," cuando vocaliza?

Scoring Criteria:
The child vocalizes four different syllables, such as "ma, da, ga, ba" or any combination of a consonant and vowel.

Testing Tip:
This item may be scored in conjunction with Item 14 of Language Expression on page 141.

23 Vocalizes a two-syllable combination

Does the child vocalize a two-syllable consonant and vowel combination?

Observe:
Observe the child's spontaneous vocalizations during the evaluation. Note if the child makes two-syllable consonant and vowel combinations.

Elicit:
Attempt to have a vocal exchange with the child. Talk, babble, coo, or produce other vocalizations to the child, or imitate the child's vocalizations. Make a list of the vocalizations the child produces.

Report:
• Describe two-syllable sounds your child makes, such as "dada."
  Describa sonidos de dos sílabas que su hija hace, como "dada".
• Does your child put two syllables together, such as "dada" or "baba," when she makes sounds?
  ¿Su hija une dos sílabas, como "dada" o "baba", cuando ella hace sonido?

Scoring Criteria:
The child vocalizes two-syllable consonant and vowel combinations, such as "dada, mama" or "baba."

Testing Tip:
The child's use of the two-syllable combinations "dada" and "mama" are usually not meaningful word attempts at this age.

24

Vocalizes in response to objects that move

Does the child vocalize in response to objects that move?

Materials: objects that move, such as push and spin tops, a busy box, wind-up toys, or toys the child can push and pull

Observe:
Note if the child spontaneously vocalizes in response to objects that move during the evaluation.

Elicit:
Engage the child in play with toys that move. Keep your verbalizations and vocalizations to a minimum during this time. Note if the child vocalizes in response to the toys.

Report:
- What does your child do when she sees toys that move, like a wind-up mobile or a pull toy?
  ¿Qué hace su hija cuando ve juguetes que se mueven, como un móbil de cuerda o un juguete de halar?
- Does your child make sounds when she sees toys that move?
  ¿Su hija hace sonidos cuando ve un juguete que se mueve?

Scoring Criteria:
The child vocalizes in response to objects that move.

Testing Tip:
Encourage the caregiver to create her own pull toys if needed by tying a short string to an object with wheels or to an object that rolls.

25

Imitates duplicated syllables

Does the child imitate duplicated syllables when vocalizing?

Observe:
Make a list of the vocalizations the child spontaneously imitates during the evaluation.

Elicit:
Attempt to engage the child in a vocal exchange. Model two-syllable combinations, such as "dada" or "baba." Make a list of the sounds and sound combinations the child imitates.

Report:
- What sound combinations can your child imitate?
  ¿Qué combinaciones de sonidos puede imitar su hija?
- Does your child imitate sound combinations, such as "dada" or "baba," when you say them first?
  ¿Su hija imita combinaciones de sonidos como "dada" o "baba" cuando usted los dice primera?

Scoring Criteria:
The child imitates a duplicated syllable, such as "dada" or "baba." These syllables typically contain early developing front consonant sounds, such as /d, m/ or /b/.

Testing Tip:
Listen to the child's vocalizations and note the sounds she spontaneously produces. Use these same sounds in the combinations you model for the child as you attempt to get her to imitate you.

26

Vocalizes during games

Does the child vocalize during simple games, like "Patty-cake" or "So Big"?

Elicit:
Ask the caregiver to describe the child's favorite games that make her vocalize most often. Try to play one of these games with the child, or ask the caregiver to engage the child in these games. Note if the child vocalizes during the game.

Report:
- How does your child participate with you in a familiar game, such as "Patty-cake" or "So Big"?
  ¿Cómo participa su hija con usted en un juego familiar como "Tortillitas" o "Aserrín, aserrán"?
- Does your child make sounds when she plays games with you like "Patty-cake" or "So Big"?
  ¿Su hija hace sonidos cuando juega juegos con usted, como "Tortillitas" o "Aserrín, aserrán"?

Scoring Criteria:
The child vocalizes during simple games like "Patty-cake" and "So Big."

Testing Tip:
This item may be scored in conjunction with Item 14 of Play on page 76.

27

Sings along with a familiar song

Does the child try to sing along with a familiar song sung by the caregiver?

Report:
- What does your child do when you sing a familiar song to her?
  ¿Qué hace su hija cuando usted le canta una canción familiar?
- Does your child try to sing along with you during a familiar song by making sounds or imitating a part of the melody?
  ¿Su hija trata de cantar con usted una canción familiar haciendo sonidos o imitando parte de la melodía?

Scoring Criteria:
The child tries to sing along with a familiar song sung by the caregiver. The child may imitate a familiar vocalization within the song or try to imitate some of the melody of the song.

28

Shouts or vocalizes to gain attention

Does the child shout or vocalize to gain the attention of others?

Observe:
Observe the child's spontaneous vocalizations during the evaluation. Note if she shouts or vocalizes to gain attention.

Elicit:
Place the child away from the center of activity in the testing area. The caregiver should remain in the child's view but not attend to the child. Note the child's reaction.

Report:
- What does your child do to get your attention?
  ¿Qué hace su hija para llamar su atención?
- Does your child shout or make loud sounds to get your attention?
  ¿Su hija grita o hace sonidos en voz alta para llamar su atención?

Scoring Criteria:
The child shouts or vocalizes to gain the attention of others.

Testing Tip:
This item may be scored in conjunction with Item 12 of Pragmatics on page 46.

29   Says "mama" or "dada" meaningfully

Does the child say "mama" or "dada" as a specific name for her mother, father or primary caregivers?

Observe:
Observe the child's spontaneous verbalizations during the evaluation. Note if the child says "mama" or "dada" during the evaluation.

Report:
* Does your child have names she uses just for you and her father?
  ¿Su hija tiene nombres que usa sólo para usted y el papá?
* Does your child call you "mama"? Does she call anyone else "mama" or "dada"?
  ¿Su hija le llama "mamá"? Ella le llama a alguien más "mamá" o "papá"?

Scoring Criteria:
The child uses "mama" as a specific name for her mother or primary female caregiver or "dada" as a specific name for her father or primary male caregiver. She does not continue to call other females "mama" or call other males "dada."

30   Imitates consonant and vowel combinations

Does the child imitate consonant and vowel combinations?

Observe:
Make a list of the consonant and vowel combinations the child spontaneously imitates during the evaluation.

Elicit:
Try to have a vocal exchange with the child. Model consonant and vowel combinations, such as "da, na, ta, ma, ga," or "ba." Make a list of the different consonant and vowel combinations the child imitates.

Report:
* What sound combinations can your child imitate?
  ¿Qué combinaciones de sonidos puede imitar su hija?
* Does your child imitate sound combinations such as "da, na, ta," or "ga" when you say them first?
  ¿Su hija puede imitate combinaciones de sonidos como "da, na, ta" o "ga" cuando usted los dice primero?

Scoring Criteria:
The child imitates a wider range of consonant and vowel combinations from an adult's model.

31 Imitates non-speech sounds

Does the child imitate non-speech sounds?

Materials: common noise-producing toys, like a drum, an animal and a telephone

Observe:
Make a list of the non-speech sounds the child spontaneously imitates during the evaluation.

Elicit:
Engage the child in play. Model non-speech sounds associated with the toys, like a cat's meow, a telephone's ring, or the banging of a drum. Prompt the child to imitate the sounds as needed. Make a list of the sounds the child imitates.

Report:
- What animal noises, household sounds or sounds of musical instruments does your child imitate?
  ¿Qué sonidos de animales, sonidos de la casa o sonidos de instrumentos musicales puede imitar su hija?
- Does your child imitate animal sounds, household noises or the sounds of musical instruments?
  ¿Su hija imita sonidos de animales, ruidos de la casa o sonidos de instrumentos musicales?

Scoring Criteria:
The child imitates non-speech sounds, such as animal noises, musical instruments or household sounds.

32 Vocalizes with intent frequently

Does the child use intentional vocalizations frequently?

Report:
- What sounds does your child use to let you know what she needs or wants?
  ¿Qué sonidos hace su hija para dejarle saber lo que quiere o necesita?
- Does she use these sounds often?
  ¿Usa estos sonidos amenudo?
- Does your child often use sounds, such as shouting and whining, to get your attention or let you know what she wants?
  ¿Su hija usa amenudo sonidos como gritar o quejarse para llamar su atención o dejarle saber lo que quiere?

Scoring Criteria:
The caregiver reports the child uses intentional vocalizations frequently. The child may shout to gain attention or whines with a purpose.

33 Uses a word to call a person

Does the child use a word to call a person?

Observe:
Note if the child calls to her caregiver or siblings during the evaluation.

Report:
• How does your child call to you or to other family members?
  ¿Cómo llama su hija su atención y la de otros miembros familiares?
• Does your child call to people by trying to say their name or by using a certain word?
  ¿Su hija trata de llamar a gente tratando de decir sus nombres o usando alguna palabra específica?

Scoring Criteria:
The child uses a word to call to a person. The child may say "mama, dada" or an approximation of a sibling's name, or she may use another more general word to call to people.

34 Says one to two words spontaneously

Does the child spontaneously say one to two true words other than "mama" or "dada"?

Materials: age-appropriate toys, such as a busy box, a doll and bottle, balls, stacking rings, toy animals, push and pull toys, or noisemakers

Observe:
Make a list of the child's spontaneous verbalizations during the evaluation.

Elicit:
Engage the child in free play. Model short phrases about the child's play and your play. Pause frequently to allow the child an opportunity to verbalize.

Report:
• How many words does your child say on her own?
  ¿Cuántas palabras dice su hija por sí sola?
• What are these words?
  ¿Cuáles son estas palabras?

Scoring Criteria:
The child spontaneously says one or two true words other than "mama" or "dada."

Testing Tip:
If possible, include objects in free play that the caregiver reports as words the child can say. However, don't urge the child to select these toys for play. This item may be scored in conjunction with Item 38 of Language Expression on page 154.

35

Vocalizes a desire for a change in activities

Does the child vocalize to indicate a desire to change activities?

Observe:
Observe the child's play during the evaluation.

Report:
- What does your child do when she wants to change activities?
  ¿Qué hace su hija cuando quiere cambiar de actividad?
- Does your child make sounds to signal she wants to change activities?
  ¿Su hija hace sonidos para mostrarle que quiere cambiar de actividad?

Scoring Criteria:
The child vocalizes when she wants to change activities. She may whine and reach for a different toy, or she may call to the caregiver for attention when she tires of a toy.

Testing Tip:
This item may be scored in conjunction with Item 14 of Pragmatics on page 47.

36

Imitates the names of familiar objects

Does the child try to imitate the names of familiar objects?

Observe:
Note the child's spontaneous verbal imitations and word approximations during the evaluation.

Elicit:
Ask the caregiver to select several toys that are familiar to the child or that the child tries to name at home. Engage the child in play with these toys. Model the names of these toys during play. Note if the child spontaneously imitates these words during play.

Report:
- Does your child try to imitate the names of familiar objects?
  ¿Su hija trata de imitar los nombres de objetos familiares?
- Which object names does she try to imitate?
  ¿Qué nombres de objetos trata de imitar?

Scoring Criteria:
The child attempts to imitate the names of familiar objects. She consistently uses the same term for an object, although it may be only an approximation of the word.

37

Shakes head "no"

Does the child shake her head to indicate "no"?

Observe:
Observe the child's interactions with the caregiver during the evaluation.

Elicit:
Ask the caregiver to describe when the child shakes her head to indicate "no" at home. Present the child with similar requests, questions or offers and note her responses. Prompt the child by modeling a "no" head shake if necessary.

Report:
• How does your child show you she doesn't want something?
  ¿Cómo le muestra su hija que no quiere algo?
• Does your child shake her head "no" when she doesn't want something?
  ¿Su hija mueve la cabeza de un lado a otro cuando no quiere algo?

Scoring Criteria:
The child purposefully shakes her head to indicate "no." She may vocalize in combination with shaking her head.

Testing Tip:
This item may be scored in conjunction with Item 10 of Gesture on page 61.

38

Says or imitates eight to ten words spontaneously

Does the child spontaneously say or imitate eight to ten words?

Materials: age-appropriate toys, such as a busy box, a doll and a bottle, balls, stacking rings, toy animals, push and pull toys, noisemakers, or play food and dishes

Observe:
Make a list of the child's spontaneous verbalizations during the evaluation.

Elicit:
Engage the child in free play. Model short phrases about the child's play and your play. Pause often to allow the child an opportunity to verbalize.

Report:
• How many words does your child say on her own?
  ¿Cuántas palabras dice su hija por sí sola?
• What are these words?
  ¿Cuáles son estas palabras?

Scoring Criteria:
The child spontaneously says or imitates eight to ten words or word approximations.

Testing Tip:
When possible, include objects in free play that the caregiver reports as words the child can say. However, don't urge the child to select these toys for play. This item may be scored in conjunction with Item 34 of Language Expression on page 152.

39 Names one object frequently

Does the child name one object frequently?

Observe:
Make a list of the child's spontaneous verbalizations during the evaluation. Note if the child's use of one word predominates.

Scoring Criteria:
The child names one object frequently. This object is frequently a food or drink item or the name of a favorite toy.

Report:
- Does your child name one object frequently?
  ¿Su hija nombra un objeto con frecuencia?
- What is this object?
  ¿Cuál es el objeto?

40 Varies pitch when vocalizing

Does the child vary the pitch of her voice when she vocalizes?

Observe:
Observe the child's spontaneous vocalizations during the evaluation. Note if the child shows changes in the pitch of her voice.

Scoring Criteria:
The child varies the pitch of her voice when vocalizing. Changes in pitch may be obvious when she is angry, upset or excited, or when she produces sounds associated with toys.

Report:
- Can you describe changes you hear in the pitch of your child's voice?
  ¿Puede describir cambios que escucha en el tono de voz de su hija?
- Can you hear high and low tones in your child's voice or does her voice sound flat most of the time?
  ¿Puede escuchar tonos altos y bajos en la voz de su hija o su voz suena monótona la mayor parte del tiempo?

41 Imitates new words spontaneously

Does the child try to spontaneously imitate new words?

Elicit:
Make a list of the words the child spontaneously imitates during the evaluation. Ask the caregiver to identify any words on the list that the child has not previously tried to imitate.

Report:
- Does your child try to imitate new words?
  ¿Su hija trata de imitar palabras nuevas?
- How often does she try to imitate new words?
  ¿Qué tan amenudo trata de imitar palabras nuevas?

Scoring Criteria:
The child tries to spontaneously imitate new words on a regular basis. The child's imitations may be imprecise.

42 Combines vocalization and gesture to obtain a desired object

Does the child combine vocalization and gesture to obtain a desired object?

Materials: a large, clear container with screw-on lid and toys, such as a jar of bubbles or a small wind-up animal

Observe:
Observe the child's interactions with the caregiver when she wants something.

Elicit:
Engage the child in play with a toy of apparent high interest to the child. Then put the toy in the large, clear container and put the lid on tightly. Note what the child does as she attempts to get the object.

Report:
- How does your child let you know she wants a toy she can't reach?
  ¿Cómo le deja saber su hija que quiere un juguete que no puede alcanzar?
- Does your child use a combination of gesturing and making sounds to let you know she wants something?
  ¿Su hija usa una combinación de gestos y sonidos para dejarle saber que quiere algo?

Scoring Criteria:
The child combines vocalization and gesture to obtain a desired object. The child may shout to get an adult's attention and then point to the desired object, whine and hand a sealed container to an adult, or grunt and point at a cupboard containing cookies.

Testing Tip:
This item may be scored in conjunction with Item 49 of Language Expression on page 160.

43 Uses true words within jargon-like utterances

Does the child use a combination of real words and jargon-like utterances when "talking"?

Materials: age-appropriate toys, such as a busy box, a doll and a bottle, balls, stacking rings, toy animals, push and pull toys, noisemakers, play food, dishes, or bubbles

Observe:
Observe the child's spontaneous vocalizations and verbalizations during the evaluation. Note if the child uses a real word in a sentence-like vocalization.

Elicit:
Engage the child in free play. Model short phrases about the child's play and your play. Pause often to allow the child an opportunity to respond.

Report:
- Does your child jabber as if she's talking in a sentence?
  ¿Su hija barbulla como si estuviera hablando una oración?
- Does your child mix one real word with the other sounds she makes?
  ¿Su hija mezcla una palabra real con otros sonidos que hace?

Scoring Criteria:
The child uses a combination of real words and jargon-like utterances when talking.

Testing Tip:
This item may be scored in conjunction with Item 34 of Language Expression on page 152, Item 38 of Language Expression on page 154, and Item 58 of Language Expression on page 165.

44   Produces three animal sounds

Does the child produce three animal sounds spontaneously or upon request?

Materials: toy animals, such as a dog, cat, pig, cow, and chicken, or The Farmer Says See 'n Say

Elicit:
Give the child each animal and model the sound each animal makes. Prompt the child to make the animal's sound, or point to an animal pictured on the See 'n Say, name the animal and pull the string. After listening to the animal's sound, model the sound again and prompt the child to say it. Repeat this sequence with all the animals pictured.

Report:
• Does your child imitate animal sounds?
  ¿Su hija imita sonidos de animales?
• Which animal sounds does your child imitate?
  ¿Qué sonidos de animales imita su hija?

Scoring Criteria:
The child produces three animal sounds spontaneously, imitatively or upon request.

45   Wakes with a communicative call

Does the child call to the caregiver when she wakes up and wants the caregiver to come to her?

Report:
• What does your child do to let you know she is awake and wants you to come to her?
  ¿Qué hace su hija para dejarle saber que está despierta y quiere que usted vaya a donde ella?
• Does your child call to you when she wakes up and wants you to come to her?
  ¿Su hija le llama cuando se despierta y quiere que usted vaya a donde ella?

Scoring Criteria:
The child calls to the caregiver, rather than crying, when she wakes up and wants the caregiver to come to her.

Testing Tip:
This item may be scored in conjunction with Item 13 of Pragmatics on page 47.

46   Sings independently

Does the child try to sing by herself?

Report:
• Does your child sing to herself at times?
  ¿Su hija se canta a sí misma algunas veces?
• Describe what she does.
  Describa lo que hace.

Scoring Criteria:
The child tries to sing a song independently. The child does not need to sing with someone and does not need music to begin singing.

47 Takes turns vocalizing with children

Does the child take turns vocalizing with other children?

Observe:
Observe the child's vocalizations when playing with other children if they are present during the evaluation.

Report:
• Describe the sounds your child makes when she plays with other children.
  Describa los sonidos que hace su hija cuando juega con otros niños.
• Does your child take turns making sounds with other children as if they were "talking"?
  ¿Su hija se turna haciendo sonidos con otros niños como si estuvieran "hablando"?

Scoring Criteria:
The child vocalizes in response to other children's vocalizations. The children may each take more than one turn.

48 Expresses early developing modifiers

Does the child express early developing modifiers, such as *pretty*?

Materials: age-appropriate toys, such as a busy box, a doll, clothing, a baby bottle, balls, stacking rings, toy animals, push and pull toys, play hats, noisemakers, play food, dishes, or bubbles

Observe:
Make a list of the child's spontaneous verbalizations during the evaluation.

Elicit:
Engage the child in free play. Model short phrases about the child's play and your play. Pause often to allow the child an opportunity to verbalize.

Report:
• Does your child use descriptive words, such as *pretty*?
  ¿Su hija usa palabras descriptivas como "bonito"?
• Which descriptive words does she say?
  ¿Qué palabras descriptivas dice?

Scoring Criteria:
The child expresses early developing modifiers, such as *pretty*, *hot* or *dirty*.

49 Asks to have needs met

Does the child use words to have her needs met?

Materials: a large, clear container with a screw-on lid and small toys

Observe:
Observe the child's interactions with the caregiver when she wants something.

Elicit:
Engage the child in play with a toy of apparent high interest. Then place the toy in the large, clear container and put the lid on tightly. Note how the child indicates she wants the toy.

Report:
• How does your child let you know what she needs?
  ¿Cómo le deja saber su hija lo que necesita?
• Does your child use words to get her needs met?
  ¿Su hija usa palabras para que sus necesidades sean satisfechas?

Scoring Criteria:
The child verbalizes or spontaneously imitates words to have her needs met. She may say "juice" to request a drink, "mama" when she wants to go to her mother or "baby" to request a doll. The child's use of pointing continues but does not predominate.

Testing Tip:
This item may be scored in conjunction with Item 42 of Language Expression on page 156 and Item 61 of Language Expression on page 167.

50

Says 15 meaningful words

Does the child say 15 meaningful words consistently?

Materials: age-appropriate toys, such as a busy box, a doll, a bottle, balls, stacking rings, toy animals, push and pull toys, noisemakers, play food, dishes, or bubbles

Scoring Criteria:
The child says 15 meaningful words consistently.

Observe:
Make a list of the child's spontaneous verbalizations during the evaluation.

Elicit:
Engage the child in free play. Model short phrases about the child's play and your play. Pause often to allow the child an opportunity to verbalize.

Report:
• How many words does your child consistently say on her own? What are these words?
¿Cuántas palabras dice su hija consistentemente por sí sola? ¿Cuáles son estas palabras?

51

Uses consonant sounds, such as /t, d, n/ and /h/

Does the child frequently use consonant sounds, such as /t, d, n/ and /h/?

Observe:
Make a list of the child's words and vocalizations during the evaluation. Note which consonant sounds the child uses frequently in her word attempts and vocalizations.

Scoring Criteria:
The child uses consonant sounds such as /t, d, n/ and /h/ frequently in her vocalizations and word attempts. The sounds /b, m/ and /g/ no longer predominate in her speech.

Report:
• Does your child use sounds such as /t, d, n/ and /h/ in her words?
¿Su hija usa sonidos como /t, d, n/ y /j/ en sus palabras?

52 Talks rather than uses gestures

Does the child talk rather than use gestures for most of her communication?

Observe:
Observe the child's interactions with others during the evaluation. Note if the child routinely attempts to talk or imitate words rather than use gestures.

Report:
• How does your child usually communicate with you?

¿Cómo se comunica usualmente su hija con usted?

• Does your child talk rather than use gestures to communicate with you?

¿Su hija habla en vez de usar gestos para comunicarse con usted?

Scoring Criteria:
The child talks rather than uses gestures to communicate. She may continue to use gestures to complement her verbalization but not as a substitute for it.

53 Imitates words overheard in conversation

Does the child spontaneously imitate words overheard in conversation?

Observe:
Observe the child's spontaneous imitation of words during the evaluation. Note if the child imitates words overheard in others' conversation.

Report:
• Does your child imitate words she hears in other people's conversation?

¿Su hija imita palabras que escucha en las conversaciones de otras personas?

Scoring Criteria:
The child occasionally imitates words overheard in conversation.

54 Asks "What's that?"

Does the child ask "What's that?" when she sees something unfamiliar?

Observe:
Make a list of the child's spontaneous verbalizations during the evaluation. Note if the child asks "What's that?"

Report:
- What does your child say when she sees something unfamiliar?
  ¿Qué dice su hija cuando ve algo extraño?
- Does your child ask "What's that?" when she sees something unfamiliar?
  ¿Su hija pregunta "¿Qué es eso?" cuando ve algo extraño?

Scoring Criteria:
The child asks "What's that?" when she sees something unfamiliar.

55 Asks for "more"

Does the child ask for "more"?

Materials: cereal or raisins and a napkin

Observe:
Make a list of the child's spontaneous verbalizations during the evaluation.

Elicit:
Ask the caregiver's permission to give the child cereal or raisins. Put a small amount of food on a napkin in front of you and give the child one piece. Pause to give the child an opportunity to eat the food and then ask for more. If the child does not respond verbally, model "more" and give the child another piece of food. Continue this sequence until the napkin is empty or the child says "more."

Report:
- How does your child ask you for more of something?
  ¿Cómo pide su hija que le dé más de algo?
- Does your child say "more" when she wants more of something?
  ¿Su hija dice "más" cuando quiere más de algo?

Scoring Criteria:
The child verbally indicates when she wants more of something.

56

Names five to seven familiar objects upon request

Does the child name five to seven familiar objects upon request?

Materials: common objects, such as a doll, a bottle, a cup, a spoon, a key, a shoe, a sock, a block, a toy car, a toy dog, a ball, or the child's toys and personal items

Scoring Criteria:
The child names five to seven familiar objects upon request.

Elicit:
Ask the caregiver to select the objects that are familiar to the child. Then ask the child to name these objects.

Report:
• What are some objects your child names?
  ¿Cuáles son algunos objetos que su hija nombra?
• Does your child name familiar objects when you ask her?
  ¿Su hija nombra objetos familiares cuando usted le pregunta?

57 Uses single words frequently

Does the child use single words frequently?

Materials: age-appropriate toys, such as animals and a barn, dolls and grooming items, play food and dishes, blocks, toy vehicles, bubbles, wind-up toys, shape sorters, puzzles, and books

Observe:
Make a list of the child's spontaneous verbalizations during the evaluation.

Elicit:
Engage the child in free play. Model short phrases about the child's play and your play. Pause often to allow the child an opportunity to verbalize.

Scoring Criteria:
The child uses a variety of single words or word approximations frequently.

Testing Tip:
This item may be scored in conjunction with Item 70 of Language Expression on page 172.

58 Uses sentence-like intonational patterns

Does the child sound as if she is talking in sentences at times?

Observe:
Observe the child's vocalizations and verbalizations during the evaluation.

Report:
• Does your child sound as if she is talking in sentences at times?
  ¿Su hija algunas veces parece como que está hablando en oraciones?

Scoring Criteria:
The child uses intonational patterns that sound as if she is talking in sentences. The child's utterances are actually a combination of jargon-like speech, word approximations, and true words, including intonational patterns.

Testing Tip:
This item may be scored in conjunction with Item 43 of Language Expression on page 157.

59

Imitates two- and three-word phrases

Does the child spontaneously imitate two- and three-word phrases?

Materials: age-appropriate toys, such as animals and a barn, dolls and grooming items, play food and dishes, blocks, toy vehicles, bubbles, wind-up toys, and a shape sorter

Observe:
Make a list of the child's spontaneous verbal imitations during the evaluation.

Elicit:
Engage the child in free play. Model two- and three-word phrases about the child's play and your play. Pause frequently to allow the child an opportunity to imitate.

Report:
• Does your child imitate two- and three-word phrases she hears you say, like "big boy" or "daddy go work"?
¿Su hija imita frases de dos o tres palabras que le escucha a usted diciendo, como "niña grande" o "papá está trabajando"?

Scoring Criteria:
The child spontaneously imitates two- and three-word phrases occasionally.

60

Imitates environmental noises

Does the child imitate environmental noises?

Materials: toy cars, trucks, a fire engine, an airplane, and a telephone

Elicit:
Engage the child in play. Model environmental sounds, such as motor noises, sirens, and a telephone ringing. Prompt the child to imitate these sounds.

Report:
• What sounds from around the house or outside does your child imitate?
¿Qué sonidos de la casa o de afuera imita su hija?
• Does your child imitate sounds she hears around the house or sounds she hears outside?
¿Su hija imita sonidos que escucha en la casa o sonidos que escucha afuera?

Scoring Criteria:
The child imitates environmental noises, such as car and truck motors, sirens, the sound of an airplane, or a telephone ringing.

61

Verbalizes two different needs

Does the child verbalize to have two different needs met?

Materials: cereal or raisins; a large, clear container with screw-on lid; and small toys, such as wind-up animals

Observe:
Observe the child's interactions with the caregiver when she wants something.

Elicit:
Ask the caregiver's permission to give the child cereal or raisins. Put the food in the child's view but out of her reach. Note the child's response. Then engage the child in play with a toy of apparent high interest. Put the toy in the large, clear container and put the lid on tightly. Note how the child indicates she wants the toy.

Report:
• How does your child let you know what she needs?
  ¿Cómo le deja saber su hija lo que ella necesita?
• Can your child tell you at least two things that she needs? What does she say?
  ¿Su hija puede decirle por lo menos dos cosas que necesita? ¿Qué dice?

Scoring Criteria:
The child verbalizes to have two different needs met. She may say "more milk" to request a drink, "up" when she wants to be held or "my baby" when she wants a doll she can't reach.

Testing Tip:
This item may be scored in conjunction with Item 49 of Language Expression on page 160.

Uses two-word phrases occasionally

Does the child use two-word phrases occasionally?

Materials: age-appropriate toys, such as animals and a barn, dolls and grooming items, play food and dishes, blocks, toy vehicles, bubbles, wind-up toys, and a shape sorter

Observe:
Make a list of the child's spontaneous verbalizations during the evaluation. Note if the child uses two-word phrases.

Elicit:
Engage the child in free play. Model short phrases about the child's play and your play. Pause often to allow the child an opportunity to verbalize.

Report:
- How often does your child use two-word phrases?
  ¿Qué tan amenudo usa su hija frases de dos palabras?
- Does your child use two-word phrases, such as "more juice" or "all gone"? What are some of these phrases?
  ¿Su hija usa frases de dos palabras, como "más jugo" o "se acabó" (se terminó)?
- What are some of these phrases?
  ¿Cuáles son algunas de estas frases?

Scoring Criteria:
The child uses two-word phrases occasionally.

Testing Tip:
This item may be scored in conjunction with Item 63 of Language Expression on page 169 and Item 70 of Language Expression on page 172.

63

Uses two-word phrases frequently

Does the child use two-word phrases frequently?

Materials: age-appropriate toys, such as animals and a barn, dolls and grooming items, play food and dishes, blocks, toy vehicles, bubbles, wind-up toys, and a shape sorter

Observe:
Make a list of the child's spontaneous verbalizations during the evaluation.

Elicit:
Engage the child in free play. Model short phrases about the child's play and your play. Pause often to allow the child an opportunity to verbalize.

Report:
• How often does your child use two-word phrases, such as "more juice," "want ball" or "all gone"? ¿Qué tan amenudo usa su hija frases de dos palabras, como "más jugo, quiero pelota" o "se acabó"?
• What are some of these phrases? ¿Cuáles son algunas de estas frases?

Scoring Criteria:
The child uses two-word phrases frequently.

Testing Tip:
This item may be scored in conjunction with Item 62 of Language Expression on page 168, Item 67 of Language Expression on page 171, and Item 70 of Language Expression on page 172.

64

Uses 50 different words

Does the child have an expressive vocabulary of 50 different words?

Observe:
Make a list of the child's spontaneous verbalizations during the evaluation. Note how many different words the child says.

Report:
• How many different words does your child say? ¿Cuántas palabras diferentes usa su hija?
• Does your child say at least 50 different words? ¿Su hija usa por lo menos 50 palabras diferentes?

Scoring Criteria:
The child has an expressive vocabulary of 50 different words.

Testing Tip:
This item may be scored in conjunction with Item 70 of Language Expression on page 172.

65 Uses new words regularly

Does the child regularly add new words to her expressive vocabulary?

Report:
- How often does your child learn a new word?
  ¿Qué tan amenudo aprende su hija una palabra nueva?
- Does your child use new words on a regular basis?
  ¿Su hija usa palabras nuevas de una forma regular?

Scoring Criteria:
The caregiver reports the child's use of new vocabulary words is consistently observed over time.

66 Relates personal experiences

Does the child try to relate personal experiences to the caregiver?

Report:
- How does your child tell you about things that happen to her when she isn't with you?
  ¿Cómo le dice su hija cosas que le pasaron cuando no está con usted?
- Does your child try to tell you about things that happen to her when she isn't with you?
  ¿Su hija trata de decirle sobre cosas que le pasaron cuando no estuvo con usted?

Scoring Criteria:
The child attempts to relate personal experiences to the caregiver using a combination of jargon and words. The child may come in from playing outside to show the caregiver a cut and try to tell her what happened.

67

Uses three-word phrases occasionally

Does the child use three-word phrases occasionally?

Materials: age-appropriate toys, such as animals and a barn, dolls and grooming items, play food and dishes, housekeeping items, blocks, toy vehicles, bubbles, wind-up toys, a shape sorter, puzzles, and books

Observe:
Make a list of the child's spontaneous verbalizations during the evaluation. Note if the child uses three-word phrases.

Elicit:
Engage the child in free play. Model short phrases about the child's play and your play. Pause often to allow the child an opportunity to verbalize.

Report:
• Does your child occasionally use three-word phrases, such as "want more juice"?
¿Su hija usa ocasionalmente frases de tres palabras, como "quiero más jugo"?
• What are some of these phrases?
¿Cuáles son algunas de estas frases?

Scoring Criteria:
The child uses three-word phrases occasionally.

Testing Tip:
This item may be scored in conjunction with Item 63 of Language Expression on page 169 and Item 72 of Language Expression on page 173.

68

Refers to self by name

Does the child refer to herself by name?

Observe:
Make a list of the child's spontaneous verbalizations during the evaluation. Note how the child refers to herself.

Report:
• How does your child refer to herself when she is playing with you?
¿Cómo se refiere su hija a sí misma cuando juega con usted?
• Does your child refer to herself by name?
¿Su hija se refiere a sí misma por su nombre?

Scoring Criteria:
The child refers to herself by name occasionally.

69 Uses early pronouns occasionally

Does the child occasionally use early developing pronouns, such as *I, me* and *you*?

Observe:
Make a list of the child's spontaneous verbalizations during the evaluation. Note if the child uses any pronouns.

Report:
* Does your child use pronouns such as *I* or *you* to talk about herself or another person?
  ¿Su hija usa pronombres como "yo" o "tú" para hablar de sí misma o de otra persona?
* Which pronouns does she use?
  ¿Qué pronombres usa?

Scoring Criteria:
The child uses early developing pronouns occasionally. The child may show confusion in her use of pronouns at times.

Testing Tip:
Use the word list on pages 21 or 22 or on the Parent Questionnaire to help complete this item by report. Note if these pronouns are circled on the list. This item may be scored in conjunction with Item 77 of Language Expression on page 176.

70 Uses a mean length of 1.25–1.50 morphemes per utterance

Does the child use a mean length of 1.25–1.50 morphemes per utterance?

Materials: age-appropriate toys, such as animals and a barn, dolls and grooming items, play food and dishes, housekeeping items, blocks, toy vehicles, bubbles, wind-up toys, a shape sorter, books, and puzzles

Elicit:
Ask the caregiver to engage the child in play and observe them, or directly engage the child in play. Model phrases about the child's play and your play. Pause often to allow the child to respond. Try to compile a sample of 50 of the child's spontaneous utterances. Then compute the mean length of morphemes per utterance by totaling the number of morphemes in all of the utterances in the sample and dividing this number by the number of utterances in the sample.

Scoring Criteria:
The child evidences a mean length of 1.25–1.50 morphemes per utterance.

Testing Tip:
This item may be scored in conjunction with Item 62 of Language Expression on page 168 and Item 63 of Language Expression on page 169.

For information on computing the child's mean length of morphemes per utterance, see page 25.

71

Imitates two numbers or unrelated words upon request

Does the child imitate a series of two numbers or unrelated words upon request?

Elicit:
Ask the child to imitate a series of two numbers, such as "five, one," or two unrelated words, such as "chair, spoon."

Report:
- How many numbers or words can your child imitate?
  ¿Cuántos números o palabras puede imitar su hija?
- Can your child imitate two numbers, such as "five, one" or two unrelated words, such as "chair, spoon"?
  ¿Su hija puede imitar dos números, como "cinco, uno" o palabras que no se relacionan, como "silla, cuchara"?

Scoring Criteria:
The child consistently imitates a series of two numbers or unrelated words.

72

Uses three-word phrases frequently

Does the child use three-word phrases frequently?

Materials: age-appropriate toys, such as animals and a barn, dolls and grooming items, play food and dishes, blocks, toy vehicles, bubbles, wind-up toys, a shape sorter, puzzles, and books

Observe:
Make a list of the child's spontaneous verbalizations during the evaluation. Note if the child uses three-word phrases.

Elicit:
Engage the child in free play. Model phrases about the child's play and your play. Pause frequently to allow the child an opportunity to verbalize.

Report:
- How often does your child use three-word phrases, such as "want more juice" or "mommy go outside"? What are some of these phrases?
  ¿Qué tan amenudo usa su hija frases de tres palabras, como "quiero más jugo" o "mami ir afuera"? ¿Cuáles son algunas de estas frases?

Scoring Criteria:
The child uses three-word phrases frequently.

Testing Tip:
This item may be scored in conjunction with Item 67 of Language Expression on page 171, Item 70 of Language Expression on page 172, Item 75 of Language Expression on page 175, and Item 81 of Language Expression on page 179.

73   Asks for assistance with personal needs

Does the child ask for assistance with personal needs, such as toileting and hand washing?

Observe:
Note if the child asks the caregiver for assistance with toileting during the evaluation.

Report:
- How does your child let you know she needs help with toileting or with washing her hands?
  ¿Cómo le deja saber su hija que necesita ayuda para ir al baño o lavarse las manos?
- Does your child use words and phrases to ask you for help with toileting or washing her hands?
  ¿Su hija usa palabras o frases para pedirle ayuda para ir al baño o lavarse las manos?

Scoring Criteria:
The child asks for assistance with personal needs using primarily verbalization.

74   Uses action words

Does the child use action words?

Materials: a ball or a doll

Observe:
Make a list of the child's spontaneous verbalizations during the evaluation. Note if the child uses action words.

Elicit:
Perform actions with the ball or doll and ask the child to name the actions. You might ask the child to name actions, such as *kick*, *throw* or *roll* with the ball or *sit*, *eat*, *cry* and *sleep* with the doll.

Report:
- How many different action words, such as *eat*, *kick* or *kiss*, does your child use?
  ¿Cuántas palabras de acción (verbos), como "comer, patear" o "besar", sabe su hija?
- What are some of these words?
  ¿Quáles son algunas de estas palabras?
- Does your child use action words, such as *eat*, *kick* or *kiss*?
  ¿Su hija usa palabras de acción (verbos), como "comer, patear" o "besar"?

Scoring Criteria:
The child uses a variety of action words.

Testing Tip:
Use the word list on pages 21 or 22 or on the Parent Questionnaire to help complete this item by report. Note if a variety of action words are circled on the list. This item may be scored in conjunction with Item 70 of Language Expression on page 172 and Item 72 of Language Expression on page 173.

75

Uses a mean length of 1.50–2.00 morphemes per utterance

Does the child use a mean length of 1.50–2.00 morphemes per utterance?

Materials: age-appropriate toys, such as animals and a barn, dolls and grooming items, play food and dishes, housekeeping items, blocks, toy vehicles, bubbles, wind-up toys, a shape sorter, puzzles, and books

Elicit:
Ask the caregiver to engage the child in play and observe them, or directly engage the child in play. Model phrases about the child's play and your play. Pause frequently to allow the child to respond. Try to compile a sample of 50 of the child's spontaneous utterances. Then compute the mean length of morphemes per utterance by totaling the number of morphemes in all of the utterances in the sample and dividing this number by the number of utterances in the sample.

Scoring Criteria:
The child evidences a mean length of 1.50–2.00 morphemes per utterance.

Testing Tip:
This item may be scored in conjunction with Item 70 of Language Expression on page 172 and Item 72 of Language Expression on page 173.

For information on computing the child's mean length of morphemes per utterance, see page 25.

76

Names one color

Does the child correctly name one color?

Materials: orange, purple, red, blue, yellow, and green blocks

Observe:
Make a list of the child's verbalizations during the evaluation. Note if the child spontaneously names a color.

Elicit:
Engage the child in play with the blocks. Ask the child to name the color of each block.

Report:
• Which colors is your child able to name?
¿Qué colores puede nombrar su hija?
• Can your child name one color consistently?
¿Su hija puede nombrar un color consistentemente?

Scoring Criteria:
The child correctly names one color.

77

Refers to self by pronoun consistently

Does the child consistently refer to herself by pronoun rather than by name?

Observe:
Make a list of the child's spontaneous verbalizations during the evaluation. Note if the child uses pronouns to refer to herself.

Report:
• How does your child refer to herself during conversation?
¿Cómo se refiere su hija a sí misma durante una conversación?
• Does your child use pronouns, such as *I* and *me,* to refer to herself?
¿Su hija usa pronombres, como "yo" y "mí", para referirse a sí misma?

Scoring Criteria:
The child consistently uses pronouns, such as *I, me* and *my,* to refer to herself.

Testing Tip:
Use the word list on pages 21 or 22 or on the Parent Questionnaire to help complete this item by report. Note if these pronouns are circled on the list. This item may be scored in conjunction with Item 69 of Language Expression on page 172 and Item 81 of Language Expression on page 179.

78

Uses two sentence types

Does the child use two different sentence types during conversation?

Observe:
Make a list of the child's spontaneous verbalizations during the evaluation. Note if the child uses different sentence types.

Report:
- Does your child use sentences and ask questions when she talks with you?
  ¿Su hija usa oraciones y hace preguntas cuando habla con usted?
- What are some of the sentences she says?
  ¿Cuáles son algunas de las oraciones que usa?
- What are some of the questions she asks?
  ¿Cuáles son algunas de las preguntas que hace?

Scoring Criteria:
The child uses two different sentence types. She expresses declarative sentences, such as "baby sit" or "want my drink," and questions, such as "go?" or "Daddy gone?"

79

Responds to greetings consistently

Does the child consistently respond to greetings?

Observe:
Observe the child's response as new people enter the situation and greet her.

Elicit:
Ask each member of the evaluation team to greet the child as they enter the testing area.

Report:
- How does your child react when people greet her?
  ¿Cómo reacciona su hija cuando personas la saludan?
- Does your child respond each time a person greets her?
  ¿Su hija responde cada vez que alguien la saluda?

Scoring Criteria:
The child responds consistently to greetings, such as "hi" and "bye."

Testing Tip:
It may be necessary to score this item through parent report if the child appears fearful of the testing situation.

Uses negation

Does the child use early developing forms of negation?

Materials: age-appropriate toys, such as animals and a barn, dolls and grooming items, play food and dishes, housekeeping items, blocks, toy vehicles, bubbles, wind-up toys, a shape sorter, books, and puzzles

Observe:
Make a list of the child's spontaneous verbalizations during the evaluation. Note if the child uses negation.

Elicit:
Engage the child in play. Use toys in a silly manner, such as putting a dog in a car to drive, or make silly comments, such as "I like to eat puzzles," about the toys. Note the child's response.

Report:
• What does your child say when she doesn't want something or doesn't want you to do something?
  ¿Qué dice su hija cuando no quiere algo o no quiere hacer algo?
• Does your child use words such as "no, not" or "don't" when she doesn't want something or doesn't want you to do something?
  ¿Su hija usa palabras como "no, ni" o "no más" cuando no quiere algo o no quiere hacer algo?

Scoring Criteria:
The child expresses early developing forms of negation, such as "no, not" or "don't."

Testing Tip:
Use the word list on pages 21 or 22 or on the Parent Questionnaire to help complete this item by report. Note if these negatives are circled on the list. This item may be scored in conjunction with Item 81 of Language Expression on page 179.

81

Uses a mean length of 2.00–2.50 morphemes per utterance

Does the child use a mean length of 2.00–2.50 morphemes per utterance?

Materials: age-appropriate toys, such as animals and a barn, dolls and grooming items, play food and dishes, housekeeping items, blocks, toy vehicles, bubbles, wind-up toys, a shape sorter, books, and puzzles

Elicit:
Ask the caregiver to engage the child in play and observe them, or directly engage the child in play. Model phrases about the child's play and your play. Pause frequently to allow the child to respond. Try to compile a sample of 50 of the child's spontaneous utterances. Then compute the mean length of morphemes per utterance by totaling the number of morphemes in all of the utterances in the sample and dividing this number by the number of utterances in the sample.

Scoring Criteria:
The child evidences a mean length of 2.00–2.50 morphemes per utterance.

Testing Tip:
This item may be scored in conjunction with Item 72 of Language Expression on page 173 and Item 75 of Language Expression on page 175.

For information on computing the child's mean length of morphemes per utterance, see page 25.

82 Answers questions with "yes" or "no"

Does the child verbalize "yes" or "no" to answer questions?

Materials: common objects, such as a pencil, a key, a sock, a cup, or a comb

Observe:
Observe the child's responses to questions the caregiver asks her during the evaluation.

Elicit:
Ask the child simple questions requiring a "yes" or "no" response, such as "Is this a key?" while holding a key or "Does a cup go on your head?" while holding a cup.

Report:
* Does your child answer "yes" and "no" to questions you ask?
  ¿Su hija responde "sí" y "no" a preguntas que usted le hace?
* Do her answers make sense?
  ¿Sus respuestas tienen sentido?

Scoring Criteria:
The child verbalizes "yes" or "no" to answer questions.

Testing Tip:
This item may be scored in conjunction with Item 71 of Language Comprehension on page 130.

83 Imitates a series of three numbers or unrelated words

Does the child imitate a series of three numbers or unrelated words?

Elicit:
Ask the child to imitate a series of three numbers, such as "five, one, three," or three unrelated words, such as "ball, chair, spoon."

Report:
* How many numbers or unrelated words in a row can your child imitate?
  ¿Cuántos números o palabras seguidas que no se relacionan puede imitar su hija?
* Can your child imitate three numbers or unrelated words in a row?
  ¿Su hija puede imitar tres números o palabras seguidas que no se relacionan?

Scoring Criteria:
The child consistently imitates a series of three numbers or unrelated words.

84 Uses plurals

Does the child use early developing plural forms?

Materials: three socks, blocks, keys, shoes, or dolls

Observe:
Make a list of the child's spontaneous verbalizations during the evaluation. Note if the child uses plural forms.

Elicit:
Present three socks to the child. Show the child a single sock and say, "Here is one sock." Then point to the other two socks and say, "Here are two ____." Pause to encourage the child to complete the phrase, or prompt the child to complete the phrase. Continue this sequence with the other objects. As an alternative, point to one of the doll's eyes and say, "Here is one eye." Then point to both eyes and say, "Here are two ____." Pause to encourage the child to complete the phrase or prompt the child to complete the phrase.

Report:
• Does your child use an /s/ or /z/ sound at the end of a word to indicate there is more than one object, as in the word *eggs* or *socks*? ¿Su hija usa el sonido de la /s/ al final de palabras para indicar que hay más de un objeto, como en las palabras "huevos" o "calcetines"?

Scoring Criteria:
The child spontaneously expresses early developing plural forms, such as *-s* in *socks* or in *eyes*.

Testing Tip:
This item may be scored in conjunction with Item 81 of Language Expression on page 179 and Item 93 of Language Expression on page 187.

85 Uses prepositions

Does the child use early developing prepositions?

Materials: a ball

Observe:
Make a list of the child's spontaneous verbalizations during the evaluation. Note if the child uses any prepositions.

Elicit:
As the child watches, put a ball in, on or under other objects in the testing area. Each time, ask the child where the ball is.

Report:
- What words does your child use to tell you where people or things are located?
  ¿Qué palabras usa su hija para decirle donde se encuentran personas o cosas?
- Does your child use words such as *in*, *on*, *under*, or *inside* to tell you where people or things are located?
  ¿Su hija usa palabras como "adentro, encima/sobre, abajo" o "adentro" para decirle donde están personas o cosas?

Scoring Criteria:
The child spontaneously expresses early developing prepositions, such as *in*, *on*, *under*, or *inside*.

Testing Tip:
Use the word list on pages 21 or 22 or on the Parent Questionnaire to help complete this item by report. Note if any prepositions are circled on the list.

86 States gender

Does the child correctly state her gender when asked?

Elicit:
Ask the child, "Are you a girl or a boy?"

Report:
- What does your child say when someone asks her if she is a girl or a boy?
  ¿Qué dice su hija cuando alguien le pregunta a ella si es una niña o un niño?
- Can your child tell if she is a girl or a boy when she is asked?
  Cuando alguien le pregunta, ¿su hija puede diferenciar si ella es una niña o un niño?

Scoring Criteria:
The child correctly states her gender.

87

States first and last name

Does the child state her first and last name when asked?

Elicit:
Ask the child, "What's your name?" If the child responds with her first name only, ask, "What's your last name?"

Scoring Criteria:
The child states her first and last name when asked.

Report:
- What does your child say when someone asks her what her name is?
  ¿Qué dice su hija cuando alguien le pregunta cómo se llama?
- Can your child tell her first and last name when someone asks her?
  ¿Su hija puede decir su nombre y apellido cuando alguien le pregunta?

88

Relates recent experiences through verbalization

Does the child relate recent experiences through verbalization?

Observe:
Note if the child relates an experience she has during testing to her caregiver.

Scoring Criteria:
The child verbally relates recent experiences to an adult. The child may come in from playing outside to tell the caregiver about a dog she has seen or she may go to an adult to tell what another child has done to a toy.

Report:
- Does your child try to tell you about things that happen to her when she isn't with you?
  ¿Su hija trata de contarle cosas que le pasan cuando no está con usted?
- How does she tell you about what happened?
  ¿Cómo le dice lo que pasó?

89

Uses verb forms

Does the child use early developing verb forms?

Materials: dolls, a dollhouse, and dollhouse furniture

Observe:
Make a list of the child's spontaneous verbalizations during the evaluation. Note if the child uses verb forms.

Elicit:
Engage the child in play. Encourage the child to use the *-ing* verb form by asking "What is your doll doing?" as she plays. To encourage the child to use the *-ed* verb form or past tense irregular, perform an action with a doll and then ask the child, "What did she do?"

Report:
* What action words does your child use?
  ¿Qué palabras de acción (verbos) usa su hija?
* Does your child add *-ing* or *-ed* endings to action words to make verbs, such as *walking* or *washed*?
  ¿Su hija conjuga los verbos de una manera apropiada, agregando lo que necesita, como "comprame"?
* Does your child use action words, such as *went, ate, slept*, or *bought*?
  ¿Su hija usa palabras de acción (verbos), como "fui, comí, dormí" o "compré"?

Scoring Criteria:
The child spontaneously expresses early developing verb forms, such as the present progressive *-ing*, the past tense regular *-ed* or the irregular past tense.

Testing Tip:
This item may be scored in conjunction with Item 93 of Language Expression on page 187.

90 Expresses physical states

Does the child express her physical states?

Materials: water or juice, cups and cereal or raisins

Observe:
Note if the child expresses a physical state to the caregiver during the evaluation.

Elicit:
Ask the caregiver's permission to give the child juice and cereal or raisins. Put the drink, cups and food in the child's view but out of her reach. Note if the child says she's hungry or thirsty while trying to get a drink or snack.

Report:
• What does your child say when she is sleepy, hungry, thirsty, hot, or cold?
¿Qué hace su hija cuando tiene sueño, hambre, sed, calor o frío?
• Does your child tell you when she is sleepy, hungry, thirsty, hot, or cold?
¿Su hija le dice cuando tiene sueño, hambre, sed, calor o frío?

Scoring Criteria:
The child spontaneously expresses physical states, using words such as *sleepy*, *hungry*, *thirsty*, *hot*, *cold*, or *sick*.

91   Converses in sentences

Does the child participate in conversation using simple sentences?

Materials: age-appropriate toys, such as animals and a barn, dolls and grooming items, play food and dishes, housekeeping items, blocks, toy vehicles, bubbles, wind-up toys, a shape sorter, books, and puzzles

Observe:
Observe the child's spontaneous verbal interactions with the caregiver during the evaluation.

Elicit:
Engage the child in conversation during play. Try to compile a sample of 50 of the child's spontaneous utterances. Note the child's ability to take turns talking during conversation and the length of her sentences.

Report:
• How many words does your child usually use in a sentence?
  ¿Cuántas palabras generalmente usa su hija en una oración?
• Can your child take turns in conversation with another person?
  ¿Su hija puede tomar turnos en una conversación con otra persona?

Scoring Criteria:
The child takes turns talking with another person using three- to five-word sentences.

Testing Tip:
This item may be scored in conjunction with Item 93 of Language Expression on page 187.

92   Counts to three

Does the child count to three?

Materials: three blocks

Elicit:
Put three blocks in a row in front of the child. Ask the child to count the blocks.

Report:
• How far can your child count?
  ¿Hasta qué número puede contar su hija?
• Can your child count to three by herself?
  ¿Su hija puede contar sola hasta tres?

Scoring Criteria:
The child counts to three rotely or with one-to-one correspondence.

Testing Tip:
Counting to three is another indicator of the child's developing ability to sequence verbal information.

93

Uses a mean length of 2.50–3.00 morphemes per utterance

Does the child use a mean length of 2.50–3.00 morphemes per utterance?

Materials: age-appropriate toys, such as animals and a barn, dolls and grooming items, play food and dishes, housekeeping items, blocks, toy vehicles, bubbles, wind-up toys, a shape sorter, books, and puzzles

Elicit:
Ask the caregiver to engage the child in play and observe them, or directly engage the child in play. Model phrases about the child's play and your play. Pause frequently to allow the child to respond. Try to compile a sample of 50 of the child's spontaneous utterances. Then compute the mean length of morphemes per utterance by totaling the number of morphemes in all of the utterances in the sample and dividing this number by the number of utterances in the sample.

Scoring Criteria:
The child evidences a mean length of 2.50–3.00 morphemes per utterance.

Testing Tip:
This item may be scored in conjunction with Item 81 of Language Expression on page 179 and Item 91 of Language Expression on page 186.

For information on computing the child's mean length of morphemes per utterance, see page 25.

Discussion of Performance

Interpreting Results

The results of *The Rossetti Infant-Toddler Language Scale* may be reported and used in different ways. The examiner may report the individual basal and ceiling levels for each of the six developmental areas included on the scale. This information allows the examiner to determine the child's relative areas of strength or weakness within developmental areas. In addition, any isolated items passed in the age range and developmental level immediately below the ceiling through direct administration or spontaneous observation should be noted. Items of this nature reflect emerging skills and may assist in constructing an appropriate program of intervention.

The examiner may also report global basal and ceiling age levels for all developmental areas included in the assessment. A global basal and ceiling can provide information about the child's overall communication and interaction age level to compare to the child's chronological or adjusted age. The examiner should exercise caution when using global basal and ceiling information. Scale results must be reviewed to insure that a poor performance in a single developmental area does not cause the child's overall performance to be reported as delayed.

To establish the global basal level of performance, review the child's protocol and find the oldest age level at which the child mastered all items across all developmental areas. This age level constitutes the child's global basal. For the purpose of establishing a global basal, when a child passes all items at an age level within a developmental area, she is assumed to have mastered all items below that age level. When a child passes the oldest level of items available within a developmental area (e.g., pragmatics 18–21 months), this area is no longer used to determine the global basal. In these instances, simply state the domains in which the global basal was established at the oldest level and compute the global basal on remaining domains. To find the child's global ceiling, find the earliest age level at which the child fails all items across all developmental areas.

It is important that the examiner develop a consistent philosophy of the interpretation of assessment results to use as a guide when sharing information about a child's performance on any type of assessment instrument. There are several considerations to keep in mind.

First, the child's state should be noted. Assessment results should be viewed as a "still picture" of the child's overall ability. As a result, the examiner may obtain an accurate or inaccurate "still picture." If the child was unwilling to participate, recently ill, out of sorts for any reason, or simply tired and uninterested, assessment results will be affected. Hence, the examiner is encouraged to ask the caregiver or parent following the examination, "Is what we have seen your child do today about right?" In other words, in the caregiver's opinion, was an accurate picture of the child's overall communication skills obtained? The examiner is encouraged to write the adult's response, word for word. Caregivers and parents have demonstrated themselves to be relatively accurate describers of their child's ability, however inaccurate their interpretations might be.

Discussion
of Performance

If the adult indicates that the child is able to do far more than demonstrated as part of the assessment, the examiner should write specific examples to use as a guide for behaviors to search for on subsequent evaluations.

Second, assessment results may be viewed as either *prognostic (predictive)* or *prescriptive* (Rossetti 1986, 1990, 2000). A *predictive* interpretation of assessment results asks the examiner to make long-term statements about the child's potential and future developmental achievement. Caregivers often ask the examiner to provide this type of information about their child's future development. The examiner should remain cautious of providing a prognostic interpretation of assessment results. The younger the child, the less predictive test results are of later performance. Time, spontaneous recovery of function, and maturation are on the child's side, thus making predictions difficult. Long-term judgments about a child's developmental potential, based on test results obtained early in life or based on a limited sample of behaviors, are tenuous at best. As the child is reevaluated over time, the examiner becomes better able to provide a prognostic interpretation of assessment results.

One technique that is helpful in formulating some sense of the child's potential for continued developmental change is for the examiner to note the *rate* or *pattern* of developmental change the child makes over time. The rate of developmental change observed over time does afford some measure of determination of future developmental performance and expectations. Although not infallible, noting the rate of developmental change is very instructive as well as clinically helpful. The rate of developmental change is only obtained through serial assessment. It is recommended that reassessment take place at least three times per year in order to identify developmental change and appropriately modify the content of intervention activities.

There are three potential patterns or rates of change noted as a result of serial assessment. The child may display any one of the following patterns of change.

1. In the first pattern, the developmental gap between where the child is functioning and where she should be functioning remains the same. In other words, the child is demonstrating a typical rate of developmental progress, despite being behind developmental age expectations. This pattern is called *normal/abnormal development*.

2. In the second pattern, the developmental gap between where the child is functioning and where she should be functioning widens over time. In other words, the child displays a pattern of development that falls further and further behind age expectations. This pattern, called *abnormal/abnormal development*, is not a positive sign and necessitates that potentially difficult information be conveyed to the adult caregivers. This second pattern of change is never positive and reflects less than optimistic potential for significant developmental change over time.

3. In the third pattern, the gap between where the child is functioning and where she should be functioning narrows, ultimately closing completely. This pattern is known as *catch-up growth* and is generally a positive sign. *Catch-up growth* is defined as an accelerated rate of developmental skill mastery, thus reducing the gap between where the child is functioning and where she should be functioning. Whereas abnormal/abnormal growth is generally a negative sign, catch-up growth is a positive sign. Further, the earlier catch-up growth is observed and the faster the gap is closed, the more positive the long-term potential for the child.

Finally, the examiner may also employ a *prescriptive* interpretation of assessment results. A prescriptive interpretation tries to answer the question "What is the next step for this child based on the assessment results just obtained?" This view of assessment encourages a more constructive use of results and assists in the development of an individualized plan to meet the needs of the child and family. For example, when an infant performs below expected developmental levels during an initial evaluation, a prescriptive view of assessment results may suggest that the examiner should ask the caregiver to keep a developmental log and to reschedule a reevaluation in three months. If a pattern of delay persists when the child is reevaluated, a program of direct intervention, home- or center-based, may be recommended.

Severity Rating Guidelines

Since *The Rossetti Infant-Toddler Language Scale* is not a norm-referenced assessment tool, there are no norms provided relative to the performance of an individual child within each developmental domain or across domains. In other words, the individual child's performance is compared to known developmental parameters as opposed to a group of typically developing children that served as the group upon which norms are established. However, there are helpful guidelines that may be incorporated when determining the overall severity of the child's communication delay. The following suggestions should prove helpful to the examiner in reporting results and in communicating assessment results to parents/caregivers.

Mild Delay

Within individual developmental domains and globally, if a child's ceiling level is two age ranges (i.e., six months) below chronological age expectations, the child may be considered to be displaying a mild delay in developmental skill mastery. The examiner must recall that ceiling levels are impacted by each individual test item. Hence, the examiner should appraise the parent/caregiver of the delay noted and should recommend that the child's development should be monitored over the next six months to observe and note ongoing developmental change. Pending the circumstances that relate to the child's risk status (i.e., potential reasons the noted delay is present), the examiner may choose to recommend communication-based intervention. It is helpful at this point to ask the parents what areas of developmental change have been most obvious in the child over the previous six months. Should the parents report significant developmental change, it is likely that the child is in the midst of a developmental growth spurt and intervention may be delayed for a maximum of three to six months. If the caregivers report little or no change in the previous six months, it is more likely that the child should be included in an intervention program immediately, with careful monitoring of developmental change as part of the intervention program.

Moderate Delay

If the child's ceiling levels (within individual domains or globally) fall six to twelve months below chronological age expectations, the child should be considered to be displaying a moderate delay in communication skills. It is important to note emerging skills for this child and to ask the caregivers to keep a careful log of developmental change from that point on. The examiner must recall that the development of age-appropriate communication skills is predicated upon the mastery of skills in a sequential manner. Hence, a 12-month delay for an 18-month-old child is more significant than a 12-month delay for a 48-month-old child. In this circumstance, the caregivers should be informed that the child is indeed displaying a delay in communication skills, and that the noted delay should receive immediate intervention to preclude later and more significant developmental pathology.

Severe Delay

A severe delay should be considered to be present if the child's performance, within an individual domain or across domains, falls more than 15 months below chronological age expectations. The examiner should carefully point out to the caregivers that the child's communication skills fall markedly below what is typically expected, and that this delay has important implications for later development and school performance. The examiner is encouraged to refer to the following discussion regarding reporting such information to the parents.

Information of this nature should be reported in a straightforward and direct manner. The examiner should allow the caregivers sufficient time to take in the implications of this information and ask any questions they desire. It is also important that the examiner give no unrealistic prognostic information regarding the outcome of recommended intervention. A statement such as "I guarantee that your child will grow, learn and change" is appropriate for all children, regardless of the degree or nature of their developmental delay (all children grow, learn and change).

The information provided above is designed to serve as *guidelines* for interpreting the results of *The Rossetti Infant-Toddler Language Scale*. The experienced clinician will realize that each child is different, and may choose to rely on individual clinical skills and experience in reporting results to parents and caregivers.

Parent Conference

Immediately following the infant-toddler assessment, the examiner usually shares test results and recommendations with the caregivers. This conference is one of the most important meetings that will take place between the examiner and the caregivers. It is crucial that these results be reported clearly and in terms that allow the caregivers to understand all that has taken place. However, the examiner must also remain sensitive to the amount of detail each parent can tolerate during the initial conference. Schedule a second conference with the caregivers to go over assessment results in greater detail, if necessary.

It is also important to actively involve the caregivers in the conference as soon as possible. At the beginning of the meeting, ask the caregivers for their impressions of their child's performance during the assessment. Continue to ask for feedback about the child's performance periodically during the conference. Listen to what the caregiver says without interruption. Present programming recommendations as options for the caregivers' considerations rather than requirements.

The examiner must remain aware of the emotional stake the caregivers have in the assessment results. Regardless of how many other professionals the child may have seen up to that point, the examiner must keep in mind that he/she may be the first professional to suggest to the caregivers that their child evidences developmental delays and that the delays noted present significant concern for long-term development and/or school performance. It is important to share this information with the caregivers in a professional and caring manner.

At times, caregivers may demonstrate difficulty accepting or adjusting to the information about their child's performance. At other times, they may deny the examiner's suggestions that the child is not doing what she should be doing for her age. It is important that the examiner maintain a supportive and nondefensive stance with the caregivers during this time. Sufficient time must be allowed for the caregivers to adapt to the idea that their child's development may be delayed. Once the caregivers sense the examiner has their child's best interests in mind, attention can be directed to what needs to be done for the child and away from where fault may lie. It may be necessary for some caregivers to meet with other professionals for assistance in better understanding and accepting their child's special needs.

Experience in working with families will guide the examiner in determining when other team members should be involved to help the caregivers. It is not the examiner's responsibility to convince the caregivers that there is something different about their child. Rather, it is the examiner's top responsibility to effectively communicate assessment results in an honest, compassionate and caring manner. Ultimately, it is the caregivers who will determine what they will do with the information presented.

Many factors impact the quality of the parent conference. The examiner must remain alert to the caregivers' reactions and understanding of the information shared about their child. Assessment results should be used to address the child's and family's individual needs. The examiner should provide the encouragement and support the caregivers need to promote their full partnership in the early assessment and intervention process. Caregiver involvement in early intervention is a significant contributor to the overall effectiveness of the intervention provided. Hence, the parent conference must be conducted skillfully so as to not place a barrier between parents and professionals, thereby reducing the parent's participation in intervention activities over time.

Therapy Implications

When assessment results indicate a child needs early communication intervention, a treatment program is developed with specific goals determined from the child's performance, his functional developmental levels, the clinician's knowledge of child development, and the needs of the family. *The Rossetti Infant-Toddler Language Scale* provides the information needed to determine therapy goals for six areas of communication and interaction: interaction–attachment, pragmatics, gesture, play, language comprehension, and language expression. The clinician can analyze the child's pattern of strengths and weaknesses in performance within each area and determine which skills appear mastered, emerging or absent. Then therapy goals can be developed to address those developmental skills that are emerging or absent at a developmental level below chronological age expectations.

The clinician can establish goals based on developmental expectations for each of these six areas of communication by noting where each area begins and ends within the scale. Each developmental area appears on the scale only when it is considered chronologically appropriate and ends once the area is considered fully established. For example, the Interaction–Attachment portion of the scale measures development up to 18 months; the level at which this aspect of development is considered fully established. If an 18-month-old child was examined and demonstrated delays in this area, it would be appropriate to develop goals to address this aspect of development as part of the child's intervention program. The clinician would then work with the caregivers to enhance patterns of interaction and attachment between the caregivers and the child. If similar delays were noted in the other developmental areas assessed by the scale, goals would also be developed to address these delays.

At the older age levels of the scale, overlap between developmental areas becomes more evident. Intervention strategies may also overlap between developmental areas. It would be difficult to target a play behavior for intervention apart from gestures and language comprehension as they are also a natural part of most play activities. Similarly, a therapy program targeting language comprehension could easily include activities that enhance pragmatic skills.

The clinician should consider the child's overall test results and his performance in each individual area of development assessed when developing appropriate therapy goals as part of an intervention program. Therapy activities should be designed with the understanding that normal language learning takes place in a natural context and a conversational framework. With these considerations and meaningful assessment results, the clinician can develop an effective therapy program to meet the needs of each child and family.

Appendix A

Materials needed for 0–12 month items:

a rattle
noisemakers, such as bells, clickers, cellophane,
    toys that chime
a soft or cloth ball
a butterfly ball or a chime ball
a large, soft plastic ball
a busy box
wind-up toys
toys that move, such as a spinning top or
    push-and-pull toys
an unbreakable mirror
common toy animals
a toy telephone
play musical instruments, such as a drum, horn
    or keyboard
a small baby doll
a toy baby bottle
a baby bottle
stacking rings
two large, plastic cups
spoons
a brightly-colored, stuffed animal
small wooden blocks
a small light-weight towel
a small toy car that rolls
large beads
a squeeze toy
small socks
a pair of small shoes
a tape recorder or CD player and children's
    music or a radio
a simple book with one to two familiar objects
    or animals pictured on a page

Materials needed for 12–24 month items:

a busy box
stacking rings
a large plastic ball or beanbag
common toy animals
a push-and-pull toy
noisemakers
wind-up toys
a plastic cup
a spoon
a shoe
a sock
blocks
large beads
a toy telephone
a brightly-colored, stuffed animal
toy musical instruments, such as a horn, drum
    or keyboard
balls
a doll with clothing
a doll with hair that can be combed
grooming items, such as a comb, brush and mirror
a toy baby bottle
a doll's cradle or crib
bins to store and hold toys
a toy barn
toy food
toy dishes and cookware
a toy coffeepot
a toy kettle or pitcher
an empty milk or juice carton
plastic drinking glasses
a large, clear container with a screw-on lid
a small wind-up animal

(materials continued on next page)

Appendixes

Materials needed for 12–24 month items, *continued*

The Farmer Says See 'n Say
a battery-operated toy with a hidden switch or a
    jack-in-the-box
toy vehicles and small figures to use as drivers
"dress-up" hats
a shape sorter
simple two- to four-piece puzzles
a simple children's book
a book of nursery rhymes or finger plays
a box of tissues
plain paper crayons
a toy vehicle with a tire removed, a doll with
    one eye glued shut or a dollhouse with
    a door removed
15 pictures of common objects, such as a bed,
    a shoe, a ball, a cookie, and a bus
15 pictures of common actions, such as *sleep*,
    eat, *run*, *cry*, and *kick*
cereal or raisins
(optional) a sandbox, sand, pails, shovels, and
    dump trucks

Materials needed for 24–36 month items:

a wind-up toy
a toy telephone
large beads
"dress-up" hats
a box of tissues
a shape sorter
a ball
a children's book
a small toy chest
a chair
a toy boat
a toy airplane
children's scissors
orange, purple, blue, yellow, green, and red blocks
simple puzzles
a jar of bubble soap
large and small matched objects, such as blocks,
    spoons, socks, cups, shoes, or balls
a variety of common objects, such as a pencil,
    crayons, paper, a key, a sock, a comb, cereal,
    or raisins
disposable cups
juice or water
12 pictures of common actions, such as *sleep*,
    eat, *run*, *cry*, and *kick*
age-appropriate toys for free play, such as
    toy animals, a barn, a dollhouse, dolls
    with clothing, grooming items, toy dishes,
    cookware and utensils, toy food, and
    toy vehicles, a garage, and dress-up clothes
(optional) a toy typewriter or keyboard

The Rossetti
INFANT-TODDLER
LANGUAGE
SCALE

Louis Rossetti, Ph.D.

Child's Name _____

Birthdate _____ Date _____

Your Name _____

Relationship to Child _____

The following questions are about your child's interactions with you and his/her communication development since birth. Please complete as many of the questions as possible. Your answers will provide valuable information for the team of child development professionals who will meet with you and your child. Thank you for your help.

Interaction and Communication Development

Do any of the following describe your child as an infant or toddler?

If you circle "yes" for any of the following questions, please use the space provided to explain.

yes   no   **1.** Was your child ever separated from you for a long time?

yes   no   **2.** Did your child require frequent hospitalization?

yes   no   **3.** Did your child resist cuddling?

yes   no   **4.** Was your child often difficult to calm?

yes   no   **5.** Was your child often colicky?

yes   no   **6.** Did your child seem very restless?

yes   no   **7.** Did your child seem very inactive?

yes   no   **8.** Was your child nonresponsive when you "talked" with him/her?

yes   no   **9.** Did your child often avoid eye contact with you or others?

yes   no   **10.** Did your child often play with toys in an unusual manner?

yes   no   **11.** Did your child use gestures to communicate?

yes   no   **12.** Did your child show interest in the people and things around him/her?
                    If you answer "no" to this question, please explain.

LinguiSystems, Inc.
3100 4th Avenue
East Moline, IL 61244
800-776-4332
linguisystems.com

Comprehension and Understanding

When you compare your child to other children of the same age:

yes   no   **13.** Is your child easily confused when there are many things taking place around him/her?
If you answer "yes" to this question, please explain.

14. How does your child respond when you give him/her directions?

15. How does your child respond to simple questions?

16. How would you describe your child's intelligence or thinking skills?

Speech and Language Development

17. Describe the kind of sounds your child made before one year of age – cooing, prolonged vowel sounds, babbling repeated syllables, squealing, etc.

yes   no   **18.** Was there anything unusual about the sounds your child made during this period?
If you answer "yes" to this question, please explain.

19. When did your child say his/her first real word?

yes   no   **20.** Did your child continue to add new words on a regular basis?
If you answer "no" to this question, please respond to a *and* b *below.*
    a. How often did your child add a new word?

    b. Did your child frequently use another way to communicate?

yes   no   **21.** Did your child's speech or language development seem to stop for a time?
If you answer "yes" to this question, please respond to a *and* b *below.*
    a. When and why do you think it stopped?

    b. How did your child communicate with you during this time?

22. When did your child first put two or three words together?

23. When did your child begin to use more complete sentences?

24. How many different words is your child saying now?

25. Do you consider your child to be talkative or quiet?

26. How does your child usually let you know what he/she wants?

If you answer with "pointing" or "gesturing" to this question, please respond to a *and* b *below.*
a. Does your child try to talk in combination with pointing?

b. Does anyone in the family talk for your child or interpret his/her gestures?

yes　no　**27.** Has your child ever talked better than he/she does now?
If you answer "yes" to this question, please explain.

yes　no　**28.** Do you think your child's speech is normal for his/her age?
If you answer "no" to this question, please respond to a, b *and* c *below.*
a. How well do you understand your child's speech?

b. How well do people outside of the family understand your child's speech?

c. How does your child react if he/she is not understood by others?

yes　no　**29.** Do you have any concern about the way your child's tongue or mouth works for speech or for eating?
If you answer "yes" to this question, please describe.

30. What concerns you most about your child's speech or language skills now?

31. What have you done to help your child learn to talk?

yes　no　**32.** Has anything about your child's speech or language development seemed unusual to you?
If you answer "yes" to this question, please describe.

33. How much time does your child spend with other children?

yes　no　**34.** Does anyone in the family have a history of any speech or language problems?
If you answer "yes" to this question, please describe.

35. List any other specialists who have seen your child:

Medical

Hearing

36. What information about your child would you most like to get from this evaluation?

Listed below are words that infants and toddlers might understand or say. Please put a check (✓) beside those words you think your child *understands*. *Circle* the words your child *says* when he/she talks to you.

all	church	go bed	more	sock
all gone	clock	go bye-bye	more cookie	spoon
apple	coat	go night-night	mouth	stick
arms	cold	go out	night-night	stop
baby	comb	grandma	no	stove
babysitter's name	cookie	grandpa	nose	swing
ball	cracker	gum	old	teeth
balloon	cup	hair	on	thank you
banana	dada / daddy	hands	out	thirsty
bear (teddy)	diaper	hat	paper	tired
belly / tummy	dirty	hi	phone	toes
big	dog / doggie	horse / horsie	pizza	toy
bike	don't	hot	please	truck
bird	done	hot dog	potty	TV
book	down	huh?	purse	uh-oh
boots	drink	I	rock	under
boy	ears	in	see	up
bug	eat	key	shhhh	want
bunny	eat cookie	Kleenex	shirt	wet
bye / bye-bye	eyes	legs	shoe	what
candy	fall down	little	sit / sit down	what's that
car	feet	mama / mommy	sky	yes
cat / kitty	fingers	McDonald's	sleep	you
chair	flower	me	snow	yucky
cheese	girl	milk	so big	
choo-choo	go	mine		

List the names of family members, friends or pets your child says.

_____ _____ _____ _____

_____ _____ _____ _____

List any other words your child says.

_____ _____ _____ _____

_____ _____ _____ _____

The Rossetti
INFANT-TODDLER
LANGUAGE
SCALE

Louis Rossetti, Ph.D.

Nombre del niño/a _____

Fecha de nacimiento _____ Fecha _____

Su nombre _____

Relación al niño/a _____

Las siguientes preguntas son acerca de las interacciones de su hijo/a con usted y el desarrollo de la comunicación desde el nacimiento. Por favor complete la mayor cantidad de preguntas que sea possible. Sus respuestas proporcionarán información importante para el equipo de profesionales del desarrollo del niño que se reunirán con usted y su hijo/a. Gracias por su ayuda.

Interacciones y Desarrollo de la Comunicación

¿Alguna de las siguientes preguntas describe a su hijo/a cuando era más pequeño?

Si chequea "sí" en alguna de las siguientes preguntas, por favor use el espacio para explicar su respuesta.

sí   no   **1.** ¿Se separó alguna vez por un largo tiempo su hijo/a de usted?

sí   no   **2.** ¿Necesitó su hijo/a hospitalizaciones frecuentes?

sí   no   **3.** ¿Resistió su hijo/a a que se le abrace?

sí   no   **4.** ¿Fue su hijo/a muchas veces difícil de calmar?

sí   no   **5.** ¿Tuvo cólicos su hijo/a frecuentemente?

sí   no   **6.** ¿Le pareció muy inquieto/a su hijo/a?

sí   no   **7.** ¿Le pareció muy quieto/a su hijo/a?

sí   no   **8.** ¿No fue su hijo/a receptivo cuando usted hablaba con él /ella?

sí   no   **9.** ¿Evitó amenudo su hijo/a contacto visual con usted o con otras personas?

sí   no   **10.** ¿Jugó su hijo/a frecuentemente de una manera diferente con los juguetes?

sí   no   **11.** ¿Usó su hijo/a gestos para comunicarse?

sí   no   **12.** ¿Demostró su hijo/a interés en otras personas u objetos a su alrededor?
           Si responde "sí" a esta pregunta, por favor explíque.

LinguiSystems, Inc.
3100 4th Avenue
East Moline, IL 61244
800-776-4332
LinguiSystems   linguisystems.com

Comprensión y Entendimiento

Cuando compara a su hijo/a con otros niños de su misma edad:

sí   no   **13.** ¿Se confunde su hijo/a fácilmente cuando pasan muchas cosas a su alrededor?
Si responde "sí" a esta pregunta, por favor explíque.

               14. ¿Cómo responde su hijo/a cuando le da indicaciones?

               15. ¿Cómo responde su hijo/a a preguntas simples?

               16. ¿Cómo describiría usted la inteligencia y la habilidad de pensamiento de su hijo/a?

Desarrollo del Habla y Lenguaje

               17. Describa el tipo de sonidos que hizo su hijo/a antes de tener un año de edad – arrullar, sonidos prolongados de vocales, balbuceo repetido de sílabas, chillar, etc.

sí   no   **18.** ¿Hubo algo fuera de lo común acerca de los sonidos que hizo su hijo/a durante este periodo?
Si responde "sí" a esta pregunta, por favor explíque.

               19. ¿Cuándo dijo su hijo/a su primera palabra real?

sí   no   **20.** ¿Continuó su hijo/a a aumentar palabras nuevas en una forma regular?
Si responde "no" a esta pregunta, por favor responda a las preguntas a y b.
    a. ¿Qué tan amenudo aumentó su hijo/a una palabra nueva?

    b. ¿Usó su hijo/a frecuentemente otra forma de comunicación?

sí   no   **21.** ¿Le pareció que el desarrollo del habla y lenguaje de su hijo/a paró por un tiempo?
Si responde "sí" a esta pregunta, por favor responda a las preguntas a y b.
    a. ¿Cuándo y por qué cree que paró?

    b. ¿Cómo se comunicó su hijo/a con usted durante este tiempo?

               22. ¿Cuándo empezó su hijo/a a poner dos o tres palabras juntas?

               23. ¿Cuándo empezó su hijo/a a usar oraciones mas completas?

               24. ¿Cuántas palabras diferentes dice su hijo/a ahora?

25. ¿Considera que su hijo/a es hablador/a o callado/a?

26. ¿Cómo le deja saber su hijo/a lo que él/ella quiere?

Si respondió esta pregunta diciendo que "apuntando" o "con gestos," por favor responda a las preguntas a y b.

a. ¿Trata de hablar su hijo/a en combinación con apuntar/señas?

b. ¿Alguien en su familia habla por su hijo/a o interpreta sus gestos?

sí   no   **27.** ¿Alguna vez ha hablado su hijo/a mejor de lo que habla ahora?
Si responde "sí" a esta pregunta, por favor explíque.

sí   no   **28.** ¿Cree que el habla de su hijo/a es normal para su edad?
Si responde "no" a esta pregunta, por favor responda a las preguntas a, b, y c.

a. ¿Qué tan bien entiende usted el habla de su hijo/a?

b. ¿Qué tan bien entienden el habla de su hijo/a personas que no son de la familia?

c. ¿Cómo reacciona su hijo/a si no es entendido por otras personas?

sí   no   **29.** ¿Tiene alguna preocupación acerca de la manera que funciona la lengua o boca de su hijo/a para hablar o comer?
Si responde "sí" a esta pregunta, por favor explíque.

30. ¿En este momento, ¿qué le preocupa más sobre las habilidades del habla y lenguaje de su hijo/a?

31. ¿Qué ha hecho usted para ayudarle a su hijo/a a aprender a hablar?

sí   no   **32.** ¿Le ha parecido fuera de lo normal algo en el desarrollo del habla o lenguaje de su hijo/a?
Si responde "sí" a esta pregunta, por favor explíque.

33. ¿Cuánto tiempo pasa su hijo/a con otros niños?

sí   no   **34.** ¿Alguien en su familia ha tenido algun problema del habla o lenguaje?
Si responde "sí" a esta pregunta, por favor explíque.

35. Nombre otros especialistas que han visto a su hijo/a:

Médicos

Para la audición

36. ¿Qué información sobre su hijo/a le gustaría obtener de esta evaluación?

Abajo hay una lista de palabras que infantes y bebes entienden o dicen. Por favor ponga una palomita (✓) al lado de las palabras que usted cree que su hijo/a *entiende*. Dibuje un *círculo* alrededor de las palabras que su hijo/a *dice* cuando habla con usted.

a?	cartera	gracias	niño	qué
abajo	chamarra / chaqueta	grande	no	qué es
abuelita	chicle / goma	hola	no hay	queso
abuelito	chu-chu	iglesia	nombre de la niñera	quiero
acabé / terminé	cielo	insecto	oídos	reloj
adentro	cocina / estufa	ir	ojos	salir
adiós / chao	columpio	ir a dormir	oso (de peluche)	sed
afuera	comer	ir cama	pájaro	shhhh
agua	comer galleta	jugo	palo	sí
arriba	conejo	juguete	pañal	sientate
barriga / panza	cuchara	leche	pañuelo	silla
bebé	decir adiós	libro	papá / papi	sopa
beber / tomar	dedos	llave	papel	sucio
bici	dedos del pie	luz	para	tan grande
boca	dientes	mamá / mami	peine / peinilla	taza
botas	dormir	manos	pelo	tele
brazos	dulce	manzana	pelota	teléfono
buenas noches	en	más	pequeño / chiquito	tía
caballo / caballito	escusado	más galleta	perro / perrito	tío
caer	feo	McDonald's	perro caliente	todo
calcetín / media	flor	mira	piedra / roca	tú
caliente	frío	mío	piernas	uh-oh
camión / troca	galleta	mojado	pies	ver
camisa	gato	naríz	pizza	viejo
cansado	globo (bomba)	nieve	plátano	yo
carro / coche	gorra / sombrero	niña	por favor	zapato

Escriba los nombres de familiares, amigos, o mascotas que su hijo/a sabe.

_____ _____ _____ _____

_____ _____ _____ _____

Escriba otras palabras que su hijo/a dice.

_____ _____ _____ _____

_____ _____ _____ _____

APPENDIX D: References

Achenbach, T., Howell, C., Aoki, M., & Rauh, V. (1993). Nine year outcome of the Vermont Intervention Program for Low Birthweight Infants. *Pediatrics, 91*, 45.

Affleck, G., Tennen, H., Rowe, J., Roscher, B., & Walker, L. (1989). Effects of formal support on mother's adaptation to the hospital-to-home transition of high risk infants: The benefits and costs of helping. *Child Development, 60*.

Als, H., Lawhorn, G., & Duffy, F. (1994). Individualized developmental care for the very low birthweight preterm infant. *Journal of the American Medical Association, 272*, 853.

Antoniadis, A., Didow, S., Lockhart, S., & Moroge, P. (1984). Screening for early cognitive and communication disorders. *Communique, 8*.

Bates, E., Beeghly, M., Bretherton, I., Harris, C., Marchiman, V., McNew, S., et al. (1986). *Early language inventory*. La Jolla, CA: University of California.

Bates, E., Bretherton, I., & Snyder, L. (1987). *From first words to grammar: Individual differences and dissociable mechanisms*. New York: Cambridge University Press.

Brown, R. (1973). *A first language: The early stages*. Cambridge, MA: Harvard University Press.

Capute, A. (1987). Using language to track development. *Patient Care, 11*.

Capute, A., & Accardo, P. (1996). *Developmental disabilities in infancy and childhood*. Baltimore, MD: Paul H. Brooks Publishing Company, Inc.

Coplan, J., Gleason, J., Ryan, R., Burke, M., & Williams, M. (1982). Validation of an early language milestone scale in a high risk population. *Pediatrics, 70*.

Donovan, W., & Leavitt, L. (1989). Maternal self-efficacy and infant attachment: Integrating physiology, perceptions, and behavior. *Child Development, 60*.

Field, T. (1981). Intervention for high risk infants and their parents. *Educational Evaluation and Policy Analysis, 3*.

Guralnick, M. (1997). *The effectiveness of early intervention*. Baltimore, MD: Paul H. Brooks Publishing Company, Inc.

Klaus, M., & Kennell, J. (1976). *Maternal-infant bonding*. St. Louis, MO: CV Mosby Company.

Korner, A., Brown, W., Dimiceli, S., Forrest, T., Stevenson, D., Lane, N., et al. (1989). Stable individual differences in developmentally changing preterm infants: A replicated study. *Child Development, 60*.

Lahey, M. (1988). *Language disorders and language development*. New York: McMillan Publishing Company.

Leonard, L. (1992). Communication intervention for young children at risk for specific communication disorders. *Seminars in Speech and Language, 13*, 223.

Linder, T. (1993). *Transdisciplinary play based intervention*. Baltimore, MD: Paul H. Brooks Publishing Company, Inc.

Manolson, A., Ward, B., & Dodington, N. (1995). *You make the difference.* Toronto, ON, Canada: Hanen Center.

Miller, J. (1981). *Assessing language production in children.* Austin, TX: Pro Ed.

Owens, R. (1988). *Language development.* Columbus, OH: Charles E. Merrill.

Paul, R., & Fischer, M. (1985). *Sentence comprehension strategies in children with autism and developmental language disorders.* Paper presented at the Symposium for Research in Child Language Disorders, Madison, WI.

Pinata, R., Stroufe, L., & Egeland, B. (1989). Continuity and discontinuity in maternal sensitivity at 6, 24, and 42 months in a high risk sample. *Child Development, 60.*

Rossetti, L. (1990). *Infant toddler assessment: An interdisciplinary approach.* Boston, MA: Little Brown & Company.

Rossetti, L. (2000). *Communication intervention: Birth to three.* Albany, NY: Thompson-Delmar Learning.

Sparks, S., Clark, M., Oas, D., & Erickson, R. (1988). *Clinical services to infants at risk for communication disorders.* Paper presented at the annual convention of the American Speech-Language-Hearing Association, Boston, MA.

Yoder, P. J., & Warren, S. F. (1993). Can the prelinguistic intervention enhance the language development of children with developmental delays. In A. Kaiser and D. Gray (Eds.), *Enhancing children's communication: Research foundations for early language intervention* (pp. 35-62). Baltimore: Brookes.